Photographer's Guide to the Panasonic Lumix LX3

Photographer's Guide to the Panasonic Lumix LX3

Getting the Most from Panasonic's Versatile Digital Camera

Alexander S. White

White Knight Press
Henrico, Virginia

Published by
White Knight Press
9704 Old Club Trace
Henrico, Virginia 23238

ISBN: 978-0-9649875-1-7

Printed in the United States of America

This book is dedicated to my wife, Clenise.

Contents

Author's Note

In October 2009, I published *Photographer's Guide to the Leica D-Lux 4*, which explains the features and usage of a Leica camera that is very similar to the Panasonic Lumix DMC-LX3, the subject of this book. I wrote first about the Leica model because that was the camera that I had at the time, and because of its near cult status with camera aficionados. I eventually realized that quite a few readers were buying the book to help them with their use of the Panasonic LX3, which is nearly identical to the D-Lux 4 in its features and operation. Although the Leica book can, I believe, be quite useful to users of the Panasonic camera, there are some differences between the cameras. Also, I wrote the earlier book before either camera had its firmware (internal computer program) upgraded, so some current features of both cameras were not discussed at all in the earlier book. I have written this book to cover the latest version of the Lumix LX3 specifically, with illustrations showing the controls and menus of this Panasonic model, and with discussion of its particular attributes.

All photographs in this book are ones that I took. The images of the LX3 and accessories were taken with a Sony Alpha DSLR-A850. All other images were taken with my LX3, with firmware version 2.2, with one exception: the photograph illustrating the Aerial Photo scene mode was taken with my Leica D-Lux 4. I will go to some lengths to take photos to illustrate a book, but I don't often have occasion to fly, and my last airplane trip took place before I purchased the LX3.

One final note about the contents of the book. I have tried my best to provide accurate information, but inevitably there may be mistakes or typographical errors that creep into the text despite my best efforts. I would greatly appreciate hearing from any readers who find such errors, or who have comments on the book. Please provide any comments you may have at http://www.whiteknightpress.com. I will try to provide errata and updates on that site from time to time.

Introduction

T his book is intended to serve as a guide for users of the Panasonic Lumix DMC-LX3 compact digital camera. Although the LX3 is one of hundreds of small cameras that have been released during the past few years, it has had greater staying power than most cameras in its class. The reasons for this longevity boil down, I believe, to basic considerations of its excellent set of features coupled with superb quality of images for such a portable device.

To put it in the simplest terms, the LX3 is a compact, unobtrusive camera with no flashy styling points, but it packs a powerful assortment of photographic features into that pocketable body.

Consider the list of features you don't find every day in a compact, non-DSLR (digital single-lens reflex) camera: RAW shooting mode; full manual control of exposure and focus; burst capability for continuous shooting; a very large (3-inch diagonal) and very sharp (more than 460,000 pixels) LCD (liquid crystal display) screen; a high-quality Leica-branded lens with a wider-angle-than-ordinary 24mm equivalent focal length and a wider-open-than-ordinary f/2.0 - f/2.8 maximum aperture; HD (high-definition) motion picture recording; excellent overall image quality, owing in part to the high quality of its "intelligent" exposure and focus controls and image processing; and excellent performance in low light, owing in part to its fine performance at high ISO (light sensitivity) levels.

Moreover, the LX3 has a CCD (charge-coupled device) light sensor that is larger than those of many other "point-and-shoot" cameras, resulting in greater image quality.

The LX3 also has a solid feel because of its metal body and classic construction. Many photographers will welcome the inclusion of physical switches to control several functions, so they don't have to navigate through multiple levels of menus to change the aspect ratio, autofocus mode, and other settings. Finally, the camera boasts a hot shoe that can accommodate powerful external flash units with the ability to communicate with the camera for automatic flash control.

Also, the LX3 includes the basic functions that all cameras in its class have: self-timer, macro mode, a wide range of shutter speeds (1/2000 second to 60 seconds), many different "scene" modes (portrait, night sky, fireworks, scenery, food, pet, baby, etc.), a decent built-in flash, and the like.

Is there anything lacking in the LX3? Some people would prefer a zoom range that goes beyond the 60mm equivalent of its maximum focal length; many would ask for a built-in optical viewfinder. Some users complain of shutter lag. The camera does not accept interchangeable lenses, and, although its sensor is relatively large for this sort of camera, it is small compared to the full-frame sensors found on some DSLRs, and cannot provide image quality to match the quality produced by those larger cameras.

But given that no camera can meet every possible need, the LX3 has found its way into the gear bag of many a photography enthusiast, sometimes to supplement a DSLR for occasions when it's inconvenient to carry a heavy load of equipment, and sometimes as the photographer's only equipment.

In any event, the camera's quality, coupled with its excellent feature set, have made it a winner by many measures.

One area in which the camera does not excel, however, is in the user's manual that is supplied in the box. Although it is very useful as a reference document, it does not always explain the steps you need to take to use a particular feature in a way that is understandable to the average user, particularly a user who is not very experienced with digital cameras.

Therefore, I felt that there was a need for a guide to the LX3 that is written in plain language, that makes the technical information in the user's manual more accessible to the photographer, and that provides some additional information based on real-world experience with the camera.

You should consult the user's manual for some information, particularly for charts of flash ranges, lists of features that cannot work together, how to connect the camera directly to a printer, and the like. This book is not a complete substitute for the user's manual.

One other note on the scope of this guide: I live in the United States, and I bought my LX3 in the U.S. market. I am not familiar with any variations that may exist for cameras sold in Europe, the United Kingdom, or elsewhere, such as different batteries or chargers. The photographic functions are not different, though, so this guide should be useful to photographers in all locations, apart from that narrow range of issues.

With those introductory matters out of the way, let's get started using the camera.

Chapter 1
Preliminary Setup

Setting Up the Camera

I will assume your Panasonic Lumix DMC-LX3 has just arrived at your home or office, perhaps purchased from an internet site. The box should contain the camera itself, lens cap, lens cap string, battery, battery case, battery charger, neck/shoulder strap, USB cable, A/V cable, several software programs on a CD, and copies of the instruction manual in one or more languages. There should also be a registration card and possibly several other notices. My box contained a notice that the software is compatible with Windows 7, and an addendum to the instruction manual discussing the updates made by the latest firmware revision, version 2.2.

Here's a small point that caused me some confusion at first. One of the items included in the box is the "lens cap string." It's not labeled, but a small loop of fabric in a plastic envelope meets that description. The little loop is thicker in one spot that's about a quarter of an inch long. The thickness is just the way the two ends of the string were joined, and the loop is supposed to remain intact. You take one end of the loop and pass it through the connector on the camera, and the other end through the connector on the lens cap. This process is a little tricky, but there's only one way to do it, so you shouldn't have any trouble.

By the way, some people have complained that the LX3 is burdened with a removable lens cap. They argue it's a nuisance because you have to remove the cap to take a picture, it may bother you as it dangles while you aim and focus, and you have to put it back on the lens when you're done. I haven't found the lens cap to be much of a bother, maybe because I'm used to using DSLRs, whose interchangeable lenses all have removable lens caps. I do see the point, though, because many other small cameras have built-in lens covers that automatically open up when you turn on the camera and close back down when the camera is turned off.

If this situation really bothers you, an ingenious user has invented a way to use an "automatic" lens cap, the LC-1 made by Ricoh, on the LX3 with some minor modifications. That lens cap stays in place but opens up like a diaphragm to let the lens poke through. You can find that solution by pointing your favorite internet search engine to an expression such as "Ricoh LC-1 mod."

Charging and Inserting the Battery

The LX3 for the United States market ships with a single rechargeable Lithium-ion battery, the Panasonic CGA-S005A. This battery has to be charged in an external charger; you can't charge it while it's in the camera, even if you connect the camera to the optional AC adapter. So it's a very good idea to get yourself an extra battery. We'll talk about that in Appendix B.

For now, let's get the battery charged. You can only insert the battery into the charger one way; look for the set of three goldish-colored metal contact strips on the battery, then look for the corresponding set of three contacts inside the battery compartment, and insert the battery so the two sets of contacts will come into . . . contact.

With the battery inserted, plug the charger into any standard AC outlet or surge protector. The green light comes on to indicate that the battery is charging. When the green light turns off, after about two hours, the battery is fully charged and ready to use. Once you have a charged battery, look for the little gray latch on the memory card/battery door on the bottom of the camera.

Battery Latch

Push the little latch to the left to spring the door, and let it open up. To insert the battery, look for the sets of metal contacts on the battery and inside the battery compartment, and guide the battery accordingly. You may need to use the right side of the battery to nudge the gray latching mechanism inside the battery compartment to the right, to allow the battery to slide in. Slide it all the way in until the gray internal latch catches above the battery and locks it in place. Then close the battery compartment door, slide the external latch back to the right (to the locking position), and you're done.

Inserting the Memory Card

The LX3 does not ship with any memory card. With this camera, unlike many others, this is not a fatal omission, because the camera has some built-in memory that will let you take a few photographs even with no memory card inserted. The amount of built-in memory is not great—about 50 megabytes (MB), which is pretty minuscule compared to storage cards of today that can hold up to 32 gigabytes (GB), or almost a thousand times more. But if you're in a situation where you need to take a picture and don't have an available card, 50 MB might be enough.

You don't want to rely on the built-in memory if you don't have to, so you need to insert a separate memory card. The LX3 uses two main varieties of card: Secure Digital (SD) and Secure Digital High-Capacity (SDHC). (It can also accept a third type called a MultiMediaCard (MMC), but only still pictures can be recorded on those cards; you can't record motion pictures to an MMC card.)

SD cards are very small, about the size of a large postage stamp. The standard card, SD, comes in capacities from 8 MB to 2 GB. The high-capacity card, SDHC, comes in sizes from 4 GB to 32 GB at this writing. What size should you use? It depends on your needs and intentions. If you're planning to record a good deal of high-definition (HD) video or zillions of RAW photos, you need the biggest card you can afford. There are several variables to take into account in computing how many images or videos you can store on a particular size of card, such as which aspect ratio you're using (1:1, 3:2, 4:3, or 16:9), picture size, and quality. To cut through the complications, here are a few samples of what can be stored on a given card. If you're taking RAW images at the highest quality in 4:3 aspect ratio (that is, the image is 4 units wide for every 3 units high), you can store just 4 images in the built-in memory, but you can store 400 images of the smallest size and lowest quality. I usually use a 4 GB SDHC card, shown on the next page. Given the conditions just mentioned, it can store 310 RAW images or 24,130 low-quality images.

If you're interested in recording video, here are some guidelines. You can fit only 6 seconds of HD video on a 32 MB card, but you can store a total of 2 hours and 50 minutes of it on a 32 GB card. You can only record up to 2 GB of video in any one scene, though. A 2 GB card will hold 10 minutes of HD video or 2 hours and 50 minutes of video at the lowest quality, QVGA-L. You're also going to run into battery problems if you try to record continuously for that length of time; that would be a situation in which you should use an AC adapter. (Note: you can't record much video at all to the built-in memory; you can record a minute or two in QVGA-H quality or about four minutes in QVGA-L quality, at 320 x 240 pixels. You can't record in any other quality of video to the built-in memory.)

Another consideration is the speed of the card. I often use a 4 GB Lexar Professional card, rated at a speed of 133x. That speed is important to get good results for recording images and video with this camera. You should try to find a card that writes data at a rate of 10 MB/second or faster to record HD video.

If you have an older computer with a built-in card reader, or just an older external card reader, chances are it will not read the newer SDHC cards. In that case, you would have to either get a new reader that will accept SDHC cards, or download images from the camera to your computer using the camera's USB cable.

Here's one more option to consider: If you want to go hi-tech, consider getting an Eye-Fi card, pictured below along with a standard SDHC card. This device functions like a regular SD or SDHC card, but it has the added capability of transmitting your images wirelessly to your computer over a wireless (Wi-Fi) network. I recommend the Pro X2 8GB version, which is sufficiently powerful to send RAW images across the network. I've tested one in the LX3, and it works fine.

Once you have your memory card, open the same little door on the bottom of the camera that covers the battery compartment, and slide the card in until it catches. To remove it, you push down on it until it releases and springs up so you can grab it. Once the card has been pushed down until it catches, close the compartment door and push the latch back to the locking position.

One note for when you're shooting pictures with the camera: when it's recording to an SD card, a red icon appears on the right side of the camera's LCD screen showing an arrow pointing to the right inside a little box representing the SD card.

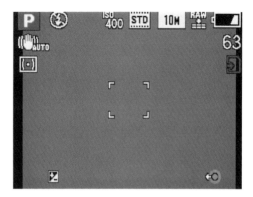

If no SD card is in the camera, a white icon containing the word "IN" stays on the right side of the screen, and, when the camera is recording an image, the red card icon flashes with the word "IN" added, showing that the camera is recording to the built-in memory instead of to a memory card.

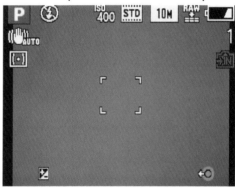

When that indicator is lit, it's important not to turn off the camera or otherwise interrupt its functioning, such as by taking out the battery or disconnecting an AC power adapter. You need to let the card complete its recording process in peace.

Setting the Language, Date, and Time

It's important to make sure the date and time are set correctly before you start taking pictures, because the camera records that information (sometimes known as "metadata," meaning data beyond the data in the picture) invisibly with each image, and displays it later if you want. Someday you may be very glad to have the date (and even the time of day) correctly recorded with your archives of digital images.

To get these basic items set correctly, here is the drill. Remove the lens cap and turn the camera's power switch, on the top right of the camera, to the On position. Then press the Menu/Set button (in the center of the array of five buttons on the camera's back). Push the left cursor button to move the selection triangle to the column for selecting the menu (Record, Play, or Setup, usually, depending on the mode the camera is in). Push the down cursor button to highlight the wrench icon that represents the Setup menu. Push the right cursor button to enter the list of setup items.

Highlight Clock Set, then push the right button to get access to the clock and date settings. Navigate with the left and right cursor buttons and select values with the up and down cursor buttons. When you're done, press Menu/Set to save the settings. Then navigate to the Language option and change the language if necessary.

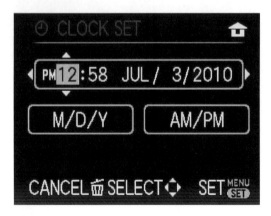

Chapter 2
Basic Operations

Taking Pictures

Now the camera is set up. It has the correct time and date set and has a fully charged battery inserted, along with an SD or SDHC memory card. Let's dive into some scenarios for basic picture-taking. For now, we won't get into discussions of what the various options are and why you might choose one over another. We'll just lay out a reasonable set of steps that will get you and your camera into action and will deposit a decent image on your memory card.

Fully Automatic: Intelligent Auto Mode

Here's a set of steps to follow if you want to set the camera to its most automatic mode and let it make all the decisions for you. This is a good way to go if you're in a hurry and need to grab a quick shot without fiddling with settings, or if you're new at this and would rather let the camera do its magic without having to provide much input. The camera will evaluate the scene and use what it believes to be the best settings to capture the scene. If the camera believes you're taking a picture of a person's face, for example, the camera should enter Portrait mode, and an icon of a face will appear on the LCD screen. Here are the steps to take to use this automatic mode:

    1. Look on the top of the lens barrel for the slide switch that selects among the three possible aspect ratios: 4:3,

3:2, and 16:9. Unless you know you want one of the other two aspect ratios, slide the switch to the center position to select the 3:2 aspect ratio for now. That aspect ratio is similar to the aspect ratio of standard 35mm film, and produces an image the same shape as the camera's LCD screen. (A fourth option is the 1:1 aspect ratio, which must be selected through the menu system, because it was added when the camera's firmware was upgraded. I'll discuss that option later.)

2. Remove the lens cap and let it dangle by its string.

3. Move the power switch at the right side of the camera's top to the On position. The camera makes a whirring sound, the lens extends outward to its open position, and the LCD screen lights up.

4. Move the Record-Playback slide switch beside the top right of the LCD screen to its up position, next to the little image of a camera. This action sets the camera to the Recording mode, as opposed to the Playback mode.

Record-
Playback
Switch

5. Turn the black, ridged dial on the camera's top (the Mode dial) so the "iA" inside an icon of a camera body is next to the white dot to the left of the dial. This sets the camera to the Intelligent Auto mode of shooting.

6. Find the slide switch on the left side of the lens barrel and notice it has three settings, reading from top to bottom: AF, AF macro (with image of flower), and MF. Slide the switch to its uppermost position, AF, for autofocus. With this setting, the camera will do its best to focus the lens to take a sharp picture within the normal focus range, which is from 1.64 feet (50 centimeters) to infinity.

7. If you're taking a picture indoors, or it's dark or shadowy enough that you think you might need the camera's built-in flash, find the little slide switch next to the word "Open" and the little lightning bolt on the far left side of the top of the camera. Push that switch to the right, and the flash

will pop open. The camera will decide later whether it needs to be fired or not.

8. Aim the camera toward the subject and look at the LCD screen to compose the picture as you want it. Locate the Zoom lever on the ring that surrounds the shutter button on the top right of the camera. Push that lever to the left, toward the W, to get a wider-angle shot (including more of the scene in the picture), or to the right, toward the T, to get a telephoto, zoomed-in shot.

9. Once the picture looks good on the LCD screen, push the shutter button halfway down. You should hear a little beep and see a steady (not blinking) green dot, indicating that the picture will be in focus. (If you hear a series of 4 beeps, that means the picture is not in focus. Try moving to a slightly different angle and then test the focus again by pushing the shutter button halfway down.)

10. Push the shutter button all the way down to take the picture.

Basic Variations from Fully Automatic

At this point I won't go into a discussion of all of the various still-picture shooting modes, except to name them. Besides Intelligent Auto, which we just described, there are Program, Aperture Priority, Shutter Priority, Manual, and Scene. There are also two Custom modes, which you can set up yourself. I'll talk about all of those shooting modes later on. For now, I'm going to discuss the various functions and features of the LX3 that you can adjust to suit whatever picture-taking situation you may be faced with. Not all of the settings can be adjusted in Intelligent Auto mode, so we'll set the camera down to the next lower level of automation, to the Program mode. In that mode, you'll be able to control most of the camera's functions for taking still pictures.

I'm not going to repeat the basic steps for taking a picture, because those were pretty basic. If you need a refresher on those steps, see the list in the above discussion of Intelligent Auto mode.

We'll start by setting the Mode dial on top of the camera to P, for Program.

You will immediately see some different indications on the LCD screen, to show that some of the Intelligent Auto mode settings have changed, because you now have much more control over matters such as picture size and quality, white balance, and others. In this mode, the camera will determine the proper exposure, both the aperture (size of opening to let in light) and the shutter speed (how long the shutter is open to

31

let in light). So in this mode you won't be making any decisions about those settings; those decisions can be made in
other modes, which we'll discuss later. That still leaves lots of
decisions you can make, though, so let's talk about the various
settings you can adjust in Program mode.

Focus

Now that you're not in Intelligent Auto mode, you have more
control over focus. Your first choice is between manual focus
and autofocus. In other words, you have the option of setting
the autofocus switch on the left side of the lens barrel to the
MF setting, for manual focus. You also have the ability to select which of several types of autofocus operation you want
the camera to use.

Autofocus

I'll discuss the various autofocus modes later in some detail.
Here we'll use the camera's menu system to make sure a standard autofocus mode is selected.

To enter the menu system, locate the circular array of five buttons to the right of the LCD screen.

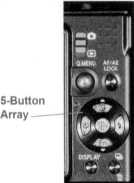

The center button is marked Menu/Set. Press in on that button and you will see the menus. You navigate through the menus with the five buttons, as well as the button at the lower right of the camera's back, next to a trash can icon. The button beside the trash can icon, in this context, acts as a "cancel" button.

When the menu system first comes up, you should see the Film Mode setting on the Recording menu. Press the down cursor button (the one directly below the Menu/Set button) several times to navigate down to the line that says AF Mode. Press the right cursor button (the one directly to the right of the Menu/Set button) to navigate to a sub-menu that shows an array of the various autofocus modes. You navigate among those modes by using the up and down cursor buttons.

Go ahead and select the next-to-bottom icon in the vertical array of autofocus modes. This icon is a rectangle with a smaller rectangle inside it. You may need to consult the user's manual at page 82 to translate these icons; this one means "1-area."

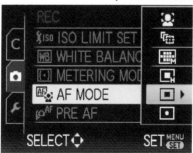

In this mode, the camera will autofocus based on whatever is shown in the one area in the center of the screen. If you want to get a bit fancier, once you have moved to this icon, you can press the right cursor button, which will take you to a screen where you can move the focusing box around (using the little joystick or the cursor buttons) and place it where you want it over the image. If you don't want to do that, then go ahead and press the Menu/Set button to select the "1-area" autofocus mode and exit the menu system.

Okay, we have selected our autofocus mode, which will display a basic window in the center of the screen. When you aim the camera at a subject, be sure that the focus window, outlined by four white corner brackets, is over the part of the picture that needs to be in the sharpest focus. When you press halfway down on the shutter button, if the camera is able to focus successfully, you will hear a beep, the white brackets will turn green, and a large green dot will appear, unblinking.

If you see a blinking green dot, that means the camera was not able to focus, either because the subject was outside of the focus range, or, perhaps, the subject was too difficult to focus on, as can happen with a subject that is too bright or too fast, lacks contrast, is behind glass, or is too dark. If the green brackets enlarge to a much wider size, that means that conditions are dark or otherwise difficult for focusing, so the camera enlarged its focusing area. If everything looks okay to you, go ahead and press the shutter button all the way down to take the picture.

Suppose you want to take a picture in which your main subject is not in the center of the screen. Maybe your shot is set up so that a person is standing off to the right of center, and there is some attractive scenery to the left in the scene. One way to focus on the person on the right is to use the technique described above—that is, to go into the menu system, select this autofocus mode, and then press the right cursor button so you can move the focusing brackets over to the area of the subject.

Here's another, easier way to do this. Aim the camera at the subject, then press the little button labeled "Focus," which is on top of the camera, at the far right, near the front edge.

If you press that button, you will see the focus area outlined with yellow triangles, and you can move it around with the four cursor buttons. Once you have the focus area located where you want it, press the Menu/Set button to set the location. Then go ahead and snap the picture.

There's another way to focus on a different area of the screen, and this one is probably the easiest of all. Place the focus brackets over the part of the picture that needs to be in focus (in our example, the person to the right). Then press the shutter button halfway down until the camera focuses and beeps. Keep the button pressed halfway to lock in the focus while you move the camera back to create your desired composition, with the person off to the right. Then take the picture, and the area you originally focused on will be in focus.

Finally, it's worth mentioning one more approach to the situation discussed above, in which your subject is a person standing off-center in the scene. You can set the autofocus mode to Face Detection, which is the top selection on the sub-menu of autofocus modes. In that mode, the camera will look for faces, and focus on any faces it locates. I'll discuss that mode, along with the other autofocus modes, in Chapter 4.

35

Manual Focus

For now, let's talk about manual focus, the other major option for focusing. Why would you want to use manual focus when the camera will focus for you automatically? Many photographers like the amount of control that comes from being able to set the focus exactly how they want it. And, in some situations, such as dark areas or areas behind glass, or where there are objects at various distances from the camera, it may be useful for you to be able to control exactly where the point of sharpest focus lies. Or, you may have a situation in which you have to focus on a particular, small area on a subject with very narrow depth of field, as may be the case in macro (closeup) photography.

To take advantage of this capability, go back to the autofocus slide switch and push it all the way down to the MF setting. You are now in manual focus mode. Now it's time to meet another controller; the little joystick, located below the Q. Menu label on the back of the camera, to the right of the LCD screen. Calling this stubby little knob a "joystick" may be a bit of a stretch, but at least it does move in all directions like a joystick.

Joystick —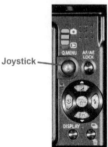

Once the camera is set to manual focus mode, all you have to do is move the joystick up and down until you achieve the sharpest possible focus for whatever part of the scene you want to focus on. The LX3 has quite a user-friendly manual focus system. As soon as you move the joystick you will immediately see either an enlarged image of the center part of the screen, an enlarged image of the whole screen, or just a normal-sized image. Whichever one you see, move the joystick up and down until you achieve good focus, then stop. You don't have to do anything else, just take the picture. (In Chapter 7 we'll discuss how you can select which of these three options is in effect by setting the MF Assist mode in the Setup menu.)

Here's one thing to watch out for: If pushing the joystick up and down does not adjust focus, check to make sure that the letters MF on the bottom right of the LCD screen are highlighted in yellow. If they are not, then push the joystick back to the right to turn them yellow. If the joystick is pushed to the left, it will control exposure compensation instead of manual focus. (Once the enlarged area appears on the screen, though, those letters will disappear.)

Even if you are using manual focus, you can call on the camera for assistance. Just press the Focus button on the top right of the camera, and it will focus for you, though you can still fine-tune the focus manually.

Exposure

Next, we'll consider some possibilities for controlling exposure, beyond just letting the camera make the decisions. The LX3's Intelligent Auto mode is very good at choosing the right exposure, and so is the Program mode. But there are going to be some situations in which you want to override the camera's automation.

Exposure Compensation

First, let's take a look at the camera's system for adjusting exposure to account for an unusual, or non-optimal, lighting situation. Suppose your subject is a person standing in front of a window that is letting in sunlight. We'll say the LX3 is set for Program mode. The camera will do a good job of averaging the amount of light coming into the lens, and will expose the picture accordingly. The problem is, the window and its frame will likely "fool" the camera into closing down the aperture, because the overall picture will seem quite bright. But your subject, who is being lit from behind (by backlight), will seem too dark in the picture.

One solution, which the LX3 makes very easy to carry out, is using the camera's exposure compensation control. Look closely at the top button of the five-button array to the right of the LCD screen.

Exposure Compensation
Button

That button, which is labeled with a little plus and minus sign, activates the exposure compensation system, which will override the automatic exposure as much as you tell it to, within limits.

Go ahead and set up your shot in Program mode and aim at your subject. Now press that top button, and a scale will show up on the screen, reading from -3 to +3 EV in increments of one-third EV. The EV stands for Exposure Value, which is a standard measure of brightness.

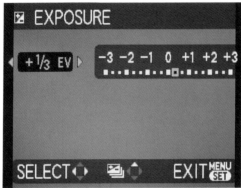

Once this scale has appeared, you use the left and right buttons to move the values higher and lower, as indicated by a little yellow box that outlines the dot on the scale that is active. If you use the left button to move the yellow box to -3, the picture will be considerably darker than the automatic exposure would produce. If you move it to +3, the picture will be noticeably brighter. The camera's screen shows you how the exposure is changing, before you take the picture.

Once you've taken the picture, you should reset the EV compensation back to zero, in the middle of the scale, so you don't unintentionally affect the pictures you take later. You need to be careful about this, because the camera will maintain any EV change you set, even when the camera is turned off and then on again.

In the example we discussed above, of the person standing in front of a bright window, if you set the EV higher by one or two notches, the backlit subject will appear brighter and likely will be more properly exposed.

In Chapter 3, we'll discuss several other topics dealing with exposure, such as Manual mode, Aperture Priority mode, Intelligent Exposure, and others.

Flash

Now let's look at the basics of using the LX3's built-in flash unit, because that is something you may need to do on a regular basis. In Chapter 8 and Appendix B, we'll discuss using other flash units, and other options for using the built-in flash, such as controlling its output and preventing "red-eye."

Here is one fundamental point that you need to be aware of: The built-in flash will not pop up by itself. If you are in a situation in which you think flash may be needed or desirable, you need to take the first step of popping up the flash unit. To do so, find the small, round slide switch on the far left of the camera's top. The word "Open" is right above the switch. Slide the switch to the right, and the flash springs up into place. Just push down on the flash until it catches again when you're finished with using it.

One point to bear in mind: Even though you have popped up the flash unit, in some situations it will never fire. In the situations in which you're likely to want it to, though, it will be ready and willing to illuminate your subject as well as it can.

Let's explore a common scenario to see how the flash works. Make sure the camera is turned on and the Record-Playback switch (beside the top right of the LCD screen) is set to Record (camera icon). Set the Mode dial on top of the camera to the iA inside the camera icon, for Intelligent Auto mode. Pop up the flash unit.

You will see the flash icon appear on the top of the LCD screen, to the right of the mode setting, which, in this case, is a small white i and a large white A inside a red camera icon (unless the camera has detected a scene type, and displays the icon for that scene, such as Portrait or Macro).

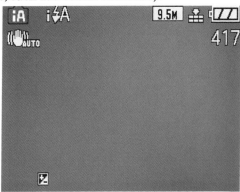

The appearance of the flash icon will vary depending on several settings, which you can choose in some shooting modes, but not others. Since you're now in Intelligent Auto mode, your choices of most functions, including flash, are limited. You will see the icon for whatever flash mode the camera has decided is best, based on its Intelligent Auto mode programming. You don't have any choice, but that's presumably what you wanted when you chose Intelligent Auto mode.

Press the right button in the five-button array on the back of the camera, the button with the lightning bolt icon on it.

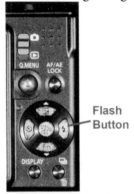

Flash Button

That button is used to select the various flash modes. You'll find that nothing happens when you press it now, because, in Intelligent Auto mode, you'll either have the flash popped up and in Intelligent flash mode (you'll see a little letter "i" in front of the lightning bolt icon at the top of the LCD screen), or you'll have it stowed away in its compartment, and you'll see the "flash off" icon, at the top of the screen. That icon is a lightning bolt inside the universal negative sign, a circle with a diagonal line through it. You can't make any other flash settings in Intelligent Auto mode.

Next, try setting the Mode dial to P, for Program mode. Now pop up the flash, and then press the flash button, on the right of the five-button array. You will find several options available: Auto, Auto/Red-Eye Reduction, Forced Flash On, and Slow Sync./Red-Eye Reduction.

You can move through this list in one of two ways—either keep pressing the flash button, or use the up and down buttons in the five-button array to move from option to option.

There's one point here that may be slightly confusing when you read the user's manual. The manual, at pages 46-47, discusses the various flash options, including the ones just listed, and a final one, Forced Flash Off. The manual makes it sound as if you can select Forced Flash Off by using the flash button, but the only way to select Forced Flash Off is to push the flash unit back into its compartment. It may be fairly self-evident that the flash is forced off when it's not popped up, but the camera still announces this fact with an icon at the top of the LCD screen. (The Forced Off flash setting has more meaning if you're using an external flash unit that communicates with the camera; we'll talk about that in Chapter 8.)

Viewing Pictures

Before we delve into more advanced settings for taking still pictures and movies, as well as other matters, we need to talk about the basics of viewing your images in the camera.

Review While in Recording Mode

Here's a quick way to review recent still pictures without having to switch from Recording mode to Playback mode. I'm mentioning this one first, partly because it's not immediately obvious from reading the user's manual.

To take a quick look at a recent picture while in Recording mode, just press the bottom, or down button in the five-button array on the back of the camera. That button is labeled "Fn," for "Function."

— Fn Button

(You can set this button to perform other functions instead, using the Setup menu, which we'll explore in Chapter 7. But this Review function is the factory setting.) Once you've entered Review mode by pressing the Fn button, you can scroll through the pictures using the left and right buttons. You can also enlarge the image by moving the Zoom lever toward the T setting. When you're done, just press the center button (Menu/Set) to exit back into Record mode. (If you do nothing, the Review mode will end by itself after about 10 seconds.)

Viewing Pictures in Playback Mode

For playback, you can leave the lens cap in place, but be sure to set the Record-Playback switch to Playback before you turn the camera on, or the camera will scold you and tell you to take the lens cap off and press the right button. Go ahead and set the switch to Playback, and, if you have any pictures in memory or on the SD card, you will see one of the pictures displayed. It will be whatever image you last displayed; the camera remembers which picture is on display even after being turned off and then back on.

To move to the next picture, press the right button in the five-button array, and to move back one picture, press the left button. (If you prefer, you can navigate through the pictures with left or right movements of the joystick.) The display on the screen will tell you the number of the picture being displayed. This number will have a three digit prefix, followed by a dash and then a sequence number. For example, the card in my camera right now is showing picture number 100-0023; the next one is 100-0024. (If you don't see this information, press the Display button to enable the information display; more about that in Chapter 6.)

If you would rather see more than one picture at a time, use the Zoom lever on the top of the camera. Move it to the left, toward the W, one time, and the display changes to show twelve images in three rows of four.

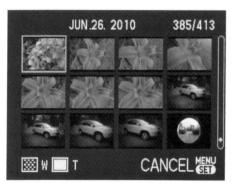

Move it to the left one more time, and it shows thirty pictures at a time.

Give it one final leftward push and the screen shows a calendar from which you can select a date to view all images taken on that date.

You can also move the Zoom lever to the right to go back through the options for multi-image viewing.

Move the Zoom lever one notch to the left to see the twelve-picture screen. Notice that the right and left buttons now move you through the pictures on this screen one at a time, while the top and bottom buttons move you up and down through the rows. If you advance to the last row or the last image, the proper button will move you to the next screen of images. Once you've moved the selector to the image you want to view, press the center button, and that image is selected for individual viewing.

Once you have the individual image you want to view displayed on the screen, you have more options. Press the Zoom lever one time to the right, toward the T, to zoom the image to twice its normal size. Press the lever repeatedly to zoom as high as sixteen times normal size. Press the Zoom lever back to the left to shrink the image back down in the same increments. Or, you can press the center button to return the image immediately to normal size.

While the zoomed picture is displayed, you can scroll around the image in any direction with the cursor buttons. Also, you can review other images at the same zoom level by using the joystick to navigate to the next or prior image, while the image is still zoomed.

Motion Picture Recording

Let's take a look at recording a short video sequence with the LX3. Once the camera is turned on, set the Record-Playback switch to Record, then turn the Mode dial to the film strip icon, for Motion Picture mode. Go to the switch on top of the lens barrel and set it to the aspect ratio of 4:3. (For movies, the only two choices are 4:3, which is what might be called "fullscreen" for a commercial DVD, and 16:9, which might be called "widescreen.") When you select 4:3, that limits you to one of three possible quality levels—VGA, which is 640 x 480 pixels, at 30 frames per second (fps), QVGA-H, which I take to mean "Quarter-VGA-High Quality," which is 320 x 240 pixels at 30 fps, or QVGA-L (L for "Low" Quality), which is 320 x 240 pixels at 10 fps. (If you choose 16:9—widescreen —then you can record in HD. Note: If you record video to the built-in memory, you are limited to recording only in QVGA-H or QVGA-L; you can't record in HD or VGA, because the memory size and speed are limited.)

You select the quality level using the menu system, as follows: Press the center button, Menu/Set, and navigate down to Picture Mode. Press the right button to open the sub-menu, and navigate with the up and down buttons to the quality you want, then select it with the center button. I chose VGA for this exercise.

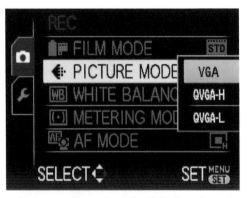

Be sure the slide switch on the left of the lens barrel is set to AF so the camera will focus automatically, unless for some reason you want to use manual focus for your motion picture. Now compose the shot the way you want it, and when you're ready, press the shutter button once. You don't need to hold the button down; just press and release. The LCD screen will dispaly the letter R along with the minutes and seconds available to record, and the camera will keep recording until it runs out of storage space or until you press the shutter button again to stop the recording. Don't be concerned about the level of the sound that is being recorded, because you have no control over the audio volume while recording.

Here's one important point: When you record a movie, the camera locks in the focus, zoom level, and lens opening (aperture) that are in effect when you first press the shutter button. So if the lighting varies or your distance from the subject changes, the camera is not going to vary its settings, or let you vary them, while the filming is in progress. Plan accordingly. Obviously this is not the best of situations for video recording; the LX3 takes nice little video snippets in a pinch, but it is no substitute for a dedicated camcorder that can alter its settings during the shoot.

One other point that's not specific to the LX3: Unless you have a good reason to do otherwise, try to hold the camera as steady as possible, and don't move it except in very smooth, slow motions, such as a pan (side-to-side motion) to take in a wide scene gradually. Video from a jerkily moving camera can be very disconcerting to the viewer.

Viewing Motion Pictures

To play back motion pictures, move through the recorded images by the methods described above until you find an image for which the screen shows the motion-picture film strip icon at the upper left. The screen will briefly display the legend, PLAY MOTION PICTURE, but that will disappear after one or two seconds.

With the first frame of the motion picture displayed on the screen, press the up button (the top button in the five-button array) to start playback. The movie will start to play. You can now use the five-button array as a set of VCR controls. The top button is Play/Pause; the right button is Fast Forward (or frame advance when paused); the bottom button is Stop; the left button is Rewind (or frame reverse when paused). Also, you can raise or lower the volume of the audio by pressing the Zoom lever on top of the camera to the right or left. You will see a little window open up on the screen with a volume display when you activate this control.

If you want to play the movies on a computer or edit them with video-editing software, they will import nicely into software such as iMovie for the Macintosh, or any other program for Mac or Windows that can deal with video files with the extension .mov. This is the extension for Apple Computer's QuickTime video playback software; QuickTime itself can be downloaded from Apple's web site. For some Windows-based video editing software, you may need to convert the LX3's movie files to the .avi format before importing them into the software. You can do so with a program such as mp4cam2avi, which is easily found through an internet search.

If you want to save one or more single frames from a movie as single images, it's easy to do so in the camera. Play the movie until approximately the location of the image you want, then press the up button, which acts as the Play/Pause button in this context. Then use the left and right buttons to maneuver to the exact frame you want. (If you want, you can press the center Menu/Set button to reach a nine-image screen, then move through it with the cursor buttons. Exit that screen with Menu/Set again.) Once you are viewing the single frame you want, press the shutter button to capture it, then press Menu/Set to confirm, and you will have a new still image at the end of the current group of recorded images. Press the down button (Stop) to exit the motion picture Playback mode.

Chapter 3
Major Features and Functions

Recording Modes

U p until now we have discussed the basics of how to set up the camera for quick shots, relying heavily on features such as Intelligent Auto mode, for taking pictures whose settings are controlled mostly by the camera's automation. As with others of the more sophisticated digital cameras, though, the LX3 has a large and potentially bewildering range of options available for setting the camera, particularly for the recording of still images. One of the main goals of this book is to remove the "bewildering" factor from the camera's aura while extracting the essential usefulness from the broad range of features available. To do this, we need to turn our attention to two subjects: recording modes and the recording menu options. First, the modes.

Whenever you set out to record still images, you need to set the LX3 to record pictures (as opposed to playing them back) by setting the Record-Playback switch, beside the top right of the LCD screen, to its up position, for Record. Then you have to select one of the available recording modes: Intelligent Auto, Program, Aperture Priority, Shutter Priority, Manual, C1, or C2. (The only other mode available is for Motion Pictures.) So far, we have worked with the Intelligent Auto and Program modes. Now we will look at the others, after some review of the first two and a brief review of preliminary steps.

Preliminary Steps Before Shooting Pictures

It can't hurt to recall the preliminary steps that you need to take before choosing any of the various shooting modes. They don't have to be done in this exact order, but this is not a bad order to follow:

- Check to be sure you have selected the aspect ratio you want: either 3:2, 4:3, or 16:9 with the slide switch on top of the lens barrel, or 1:1, which has to be set with the menu system. I generally use 3:2 for everyday shooting, but you may want to experiment to see which you prefer.

- Check to be sure you have selected the focus method you want: either AF for autofocus; AF Macro for autofocus with close-ups; or MF for manual focus. Use the slide switch on the left side of the lens barrel.

- Be sure the Record-Playback selector switch, at the top right side of the LCD screen, is set to Record, in the up position, with the camera icon.

- Remove the lens cap.

- Turn on the camera.

Now you're ready to select a recording mode. I'll go through them all below.

Intelligent Auto Mode

We've already talked about this shooting mode. This is the one you probably want if you just need to have the camera ready for a quick shot, maybe in an environment with fast-paced events when you won't have much time to fuss with settings.

To set this mode, turn the Mode dial, on top of the camera to the right of the flash shoe, to the camera icon with the letters "iA" (for "Intelligent Automatic") inside it. (Be sure to distinguish this setting from the capital "A" with no icon, which sets a different mode, Aperture Priority.)

When you select Intelligent Auto mode, the camera makes quite a few decisions for you. It sets image stabilization, quick autofocus, face detection, Intelligent Exposure, and red-eye correction. We'll discuss all of those options later in connection with Recording menu settings. This mode also sets scene detection, which means that, if the camera detects one of certain particular types of scene, it will set itself up for that scene type, just as if you had selected Scene mode and that type of scene, using the Mode dial and menu system. The types of scene that the camera will detect are Portrait, Scenery, Macro, Night Portrait, and Night Scenery. (Actually, Macro is not a scene type that's available on the Scene menu; it's really a focus setting. We'll talk about Scene mode later in this chapter.)

Also, choosing Intelligent Auto mode imposes limitations, some of which you may not like, so let's discuss those. One of the limitations I don't like is that this mode limits your Picture

Size choices to just three or four, depending on what aspect ratio you have selected, instead of the five or six that are available in Program mode. More importantly, in Intelligent Auto mode you cannot select RAW for the Quality setting, which is set automatically to either Fine or Standard, depending on the Picture Size. We'll discuss RAW later, but if you want to have the highest possible quality of images or intend to process them using one of the more sophisticated photo editing programs, like Adobe Photoshop, you won't like having to do without the RAW Quality setting.

There are many other limitations imposed by Intelligent Auto Mode. Basically, when you choose this mode, the Recording menu is limited to two choices: Picture Size, ranging from 10 MP down to 0.3 MP, and AF tracking, on or off. It may not be such a bad thing to do without a lot of choices, though, because, after all, the purpose of Intelligent Auto mode is for the camera to make quick, reasonably good choices for you so you can spring into action with the shutter button on a split second's notice.

Program Mode

Choose this mode by turning the Mode dial to the P setting. Program mode lets you control many of the settings available, though it doesn't give you full control over exposure, as the Manual Exposure mode does. (You still can override the camera's automatic exposure to a fair extent, though, by using exposure compensation and exposure bracketing, also known as

Auto Bracket.) You don't have to make a lot of decisions if you don't want to, however, because the camera will make reasonable choices for you as defaults.

One way to look at Program mode is that it greatly expands the choices available through the Recording menu. You will be able to make choices involving picture quality, image stabilization, ISO sensitivity, metering method, and others. We won't discuss all of those choices here; to explore that topic, go to the discussion of the Recording menu in Chapter 4 and check out all of the different selections that are available to you.

It is worth mentioning here that Program mode has the great advantage of letting you choose RAW quality for your still images. To do that, activate the Recording menu by pressing the Menu/Set button (the center button in the five-button array). Navigate down to the Quality setting, then press the right button to pop up the sub-menu with the five Quality settings: Fine, Standard, RAW, RAW plus Fine, and RAW plus Standard.

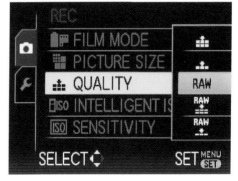

The Fine and Standard settings produce normal JPEG images. (JPEG stands for Joint Photographic Experts Group, an industry group that sets standards for photographic file formats.) With the last two settings, the camera actually records two images as noted, so you will have both the RAW and the non-RAW (JPEG) image available. This choice can be useful if you won't have immediate access to software for editing the RAW images, and want to be able to use the lesser-quality images quickly.

Besides unlocking the many options in the Recording menu, choosing Program Mode also provides you with access to many options in the Setup menu that are not available in Intelligent Auto Mode, such as various settings for the LCD screen display, including the histogram, manual focus assist, and highlight, which we will discuss in Chapter 7.

Are there any drawbacks to using Program mode? As with any choice of this sort, there are some tradeoffs. The most obvious issue is that you don't have complete control over the camera's settings. You can choose a lot of options, such as Film Type, Quality, Picture Size, and ISO, but you can't directly control the aperture or shutter speed, which are set according to the camera's programming. You can exercise a good deal of control through exposure compensation and Program Shift (see later discussion), but that's not quite the same as selecting a particular aperture or shutter speed at the outset. If you need that degree of control, you'll need to select Aperture Priority, Shutter Priority, or Manual for your shooting mode.

There is one specific issue related to the lack of control over aperture and shutter speed when you're using Program mode. When this shooting mode is set, the Minimum Shutter Speed setting will be activated; you cannot turn it off. The slowest minimum shutter speed you can set in that situation is one second. So if you are trying to take a time exposure in a dark area (using a tripod, presumably), where the correct shutter speed would be, say, five seconds, the camera will not expose the picture properly. The minimum shutter speed setting of one second will be the longest exposure possible. If you expect to have exposures longer than one second, you need to select a shooting mode other than Program. (Manual, Aperture Priority, Shutter Priority, or certain Scene types.)

Aperture Priority Mode

You set the Aperture Priority mode by turning the Mode dial to the capital A that stands alone, not the "iA" inside the camera icon. Aperture Priority mode is similar to Program mode in the functions that are available for you to control, but as the name implies, it also gives you, the photographer, more control over the camera's aperture.

Before discussing the nuts and bolts of the settings for this mode, let's talk about what aperture is and why you would want to control it. The camera's aperture is a measure of how wide its opening is to let in light. The aperture's width is measured numerically in f-stops. For the LX3, the range of f-stops is from f/2.0 (wide open) to f/8.0 (most narrow). The amount of light that is let into the camera to create an image on the camera's sensor is controlled by the combination of aperture (how wide open the lens is) and shutter speed (how long the shutter remains open to let in the light).

For some purposes, you may want to have control over how wide open the aperture is, but still let the camera choose the corresponding shutter speed. Here are a couple of examples involving depth of field. Depth of field is a measure of how well a camera is able to keep multiple objects or subjects in focus at different distances (focal lengths). For example, say you have three of your friends lined up so you can see all of them, but they are standing at different distances — five, seven, and nine feet (1.5, 2.1, and 2.7 meters) from the camera. If the camera's depth of field is quite narrow at a particular focal length, such as five feet (1.5 meters), then, in this case, if you focus on the friend at that distance, the other two will be out of focus and blurry. But if the camera's depth of field when focused at five feet (1.5 meters) is broad, then it may be possible for all three friends to be in sharp focus in your photograph, even if the focus is set for the friend at five feet (1.5 meters).

What does all of that have to do with aperture? One of the rules of photography is that the wider the camera's aperture is, the narrower its depth of field is at a given focal length. So in our example above, if you have the camera's aperture set to its widest opening, f/2.0, the depth of field will be narrow, and it will be possible to keep fewer items in focus at varying distances from the camera. If the aperture is set to the narrowest, f/8.0, the depth of field will be greater, and it will be possible to have more items in focus at varying distances.

In practical terms, if you want to have the sharpest picture possible, especially when you have subjects at varying distances from the lens and you want them to be in focus to the greatest extent possible, then you may want to control the aperture, and make sure it is set to the highest number (narrowest opening) possible.

On the other hand, there are occasions when photographers prize a narrow depth of field. This situation can arise when you need to set off your subject from the background. For example, suppose you need to take a photo of a teapot that you're going to sell on eBay, but your room is crowded with other objects that make for a distracting background. If you can achieve a narrow depth of field, you can have the teapot in sharp focus, but leave the background quite blurry and indistinct. This effect is sometimes called "bokeh," a Japanese term describing an aesthetically pleasing blurriness of the background. In this situation, the blurriness of the background can be a great asset, reducing the distraction factor of unwanted objects and highlighting the sharply focused image of your subject.

So with our awareness of the virtues of selecting an aperture, on to the technical steps involved. Once you have moved the Mode dial to the A setting, the next step is quite simple. Use the joystick (the little knob below the label Q. Menu) to change the aperture. Move the joystick up to get a narrower aperture (higher number) and move it down to get a wider aperture (lower number). The number of the f-stop will display in the bottom center of the screen in yellow numerals. The shutter speed will show up also, but not until you have pressed the shutter button halfway down, to let the camera evaluate the lighting conditions.

There's a tricky aspect to this adjustment, which is not clearly covered in the user's manual. The joystick can be used to control another function in this context, and you have to be somewhat careful to avoid slipping over into that function. Here's what I mean. If you're controlling the aperture as described above, the aperture numbers will be displayed in yellow numerals on the screen. They will change as you move the joystick up and down. But if you should move the joystick to the left, the aperture numerals will turn white, and they will no longer change as you move the joystick up and down.

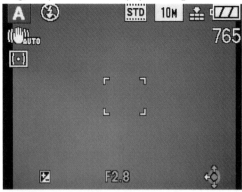

What happens here is if you move the joystick to the left, you trigger a different function—exposure compensation. That function can also be activated by pushing the top button in the five-button array, and then using the left and right buttons to adjust the exposure to make the image brighter or darker. But the joystick gives you a quicker way to make this adjustment. Once you have moved the joystick to the left to enter the exposure compensation realm, you move the joystick to increase the brightness of the image (joystick up) or to decrease it (joystick down), in the 1/3-EV increments that we discussed earlier.

There is another indicator on the screen that gives you information about what is going on here. That indicator is a set of arrows at the very bottom right of the screen. You will see either two or three arrows, depending on the situation. The up and down arrows are yellow, and the sideways arrows are white. When you see an arrow, that means you can navigate the joystick in that direction. So if you see only an up arrow and a right arrow, that means you can move the joystick either up or to the right, but you can't move it any further down or to the left.

To put this another way, if you are controlling aperture with the joystick, you will see one or two vertical arrows and one arrow pointing to the left. That means that you can push the joystick to the left to switch into exposure compensation adjustments. If you see an arrow pointing to the right, that means you are currently in the exposure compensation system, and you can move the joystick back to the right to switch back into aperture adjustments.

One more note on Aperture Priority mode that might not be immediately obvious and easily could lead to confusion; not all apertures are available at all times. In particular, the widest-open aperture, f/2.0, is available only when the lens is zoomed out to its wide-angle setting (moved toward the W indicator). At higher zoom levels, the widest aperture available is f/2.8. To see an illustration of this point, here is a quick test. Zoom the lens out by moving the Zoom lever all the way to the left, toward the W. Then select Aperture Priority mode and select an aperture of f/2.0 by moving the joystick all the way down. Now zoom the lens in by moving the Zoom lever to the right, toward the T. After the zoom indicator is done showing up on the screen, you will see that the aperture has been changed to f/2.8, because that is the limit for the aperture at the telephoto zoom level. (The aperture will change back to f/2.0 if you move the zoom back to the wide-angle setting.)

Shutter Priority Mode

The next mode is a complement to Aperture Priority mode. In Shutter Priority mode, you choose whatever shutter speed you want, and the camera will set the corresponding aperture in order to achieve a proper exposure of the image. In this case, the creative considerations are somewhat different than with Aperture Priority. The LX3 has a very wide range of shutter speeds available in Shutter Priority mode (the range differs somewhat in some other modes). In this mode, you can set the shutter to be open for a variety of intervals ranging from 8 full seconds to 1/2000 of a second.

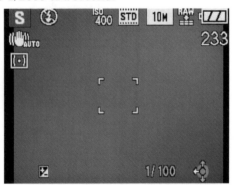

So if you are photographing fast action, such as a baseball swing or a hurdles event at a track meet, and you want to stop the action with a minimum of blur, you will want to select a fast shutter speed, such as 1/1000 of a second. In other cases, for creative purposes, you may want to select a slow shutter speed to achieve a certain effect, such as leaving the shutter open to capture a trail of automobiles' taillights at night.

The settings for Shutter Priority mode are, not surprisingly, quite similar to those for Aperture Priority mode. You select the mode by setting the Mode dial on top of the camera to the S indicator. Then you select the shutter speed by up-and-down motion of the joystick. Move it up for faster shutter speeds, and down for slower ones. The camera will then select the appropriate aperture to achieve a proper exposure, when you press the shutter button halfway down.

Once you've pushed the shutter button halfway down, watch the colors of the shutter speed number and the f-stop number on the screen. If the numbers turn red, that means that proper exposure at that shutter speed is not possible at any available aperture, according to the camera's calculations. For example, if you set the aperture to 1/320 of a second in a fairly dark indoor setting, the shutter speed number and the aperture number (which will be f/2.0, the widest setting, if the zoom is set to wide angle) may turn red, indicating that proper exposure is not possible. One good thing in this situation is that the camera will still let you take the picture, despite having turned the numbers red to warn you. The camera is saying, in effect, "Look, you may not want to do this, but that's your business. If you want a dark picture for some reason, help yourself." (Note: This situation is less likely to take place when you're in Aperture Priority mode, because, unlike the situation with f-stops, there is a wide range of shutter speeds for the camera to choose from—a range from 8 seconds to 1/2000 second. So no matter what aperture you select, there is likely to be a shutter speed available that will result in proper exposure.)

One thing to watch out for on the shutter speed display is the distinction between the fractions of a second and the times that are one second or longer. The LX3 has a good display in this regard, because it displays the fractions with a divider line, such as 1/2 and 1/125. One aspect of this display that can be somewhat confusing is that some of the times are displayed as a combination of fractions and decimals, such as 1/2.5 and 1/3.2. I find these numbers a bit hard to translate mentally into a time I can relate to. Here is a table that translates these numbers into a more understandable form:

1/1.3	0.77 or 10/13 second
1/1.6	0.625 or 5/8 second
1/2.5	0.4 or 2/5 second
1/3.2	0.31 or 5/16 second

Also, as with Aperture Priority mode, the joystick serves two functions in Shutter Priority mode. If you stick to vertical movements, you will control the shutter speed, but if you move the joystick to the left, the shutter speed numbers will turn white, and you will see yellow figures for the exposure compensation display. Moving the joystick vertically now will control the exposure compensation amount. You will have to move the joystick back to the right to get back into controlling the shutter speed with the joystick.

Manual Exposure Mode

The LX3 has a fully manual mode for control of exposure, which is one of the great features of this camera. Not many compact digital cameras have a manual exposure mode, which is a boon for serious amateurs who want to exert full creative control over exposure decisions.

The technique for using this mode is not far removed from what we discussed in connection with the Aperture Priority and Shutter Priority modes. To control exposure manually, set the Mode dial to the M indicator. Now the joystick will control both aperture and shutter speed. Earlier, we saw how the joystick has two functions in the Aperture Priority and Shutter Priority modes: controlling either aperture or shutter speed, and also controlling exposure compensation, if you move the joystick to the left. In Manual Exposure mode, you shift back and forth between controlling aperture and controlling shutter speed by moving the joystick horizontally, and you then adjust the settings for the selected function by moving the joystick vertically. You no longer can control exposure compensation, because that would be of no real use when you're already controlling the exposure manually.

To control the aperture, first move the joystick to the left. The aperture number (such as 2.8 or 3.5) will turn yellow, and can now be raised by moving the joystick up, or lowered by moving the joystick down. To shift to controlling the shutter speed, move the joystick to the right. The shutter speed number (such as 1/30 or 1/100) will turn yellow, and can now be changed to a faster speed by moving the joystick up, or to a slower speed by moving the joystick down. The joystick navigation display, with the little arrows in the lower right of the screen, will remind you which function is active. If a little arrow is pointing to the right, you are able to move the joystick to the right to select shutter speed. If the little arrow is pointing to the left, you are able to move the joystick to the left to select aperture.

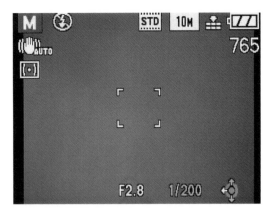

One note to remember: if you recall, with Aperture Priority mode, you cannot set the aperture to f/2.0 when the lens is fully zoomed in. The same situation is true with Manual mode: you cannot set the wide-open aperture of f/2.0 when the lens is zoomed all the way in to the 60mm equivalent setting.

With Manual Exposure mode, the settings for aperture and shutter speed are independent of each other. When you change one, the other one stays unchanged until you change it manually. The camera is leaving the creative decision about exposure entirely up to you, even if the resulting photograph would be washed out by excessive exposure or under-exposed to the point of near-blackness.

However, the camera is not going to abandon you completely, so you won't have to use a separate light meter or other external aids to gauge the correct exposure settings. Even though you have selected Manual exposure control, the camera will still provide help if you want it.

Once you are in Manual Exposure mode, either before or after you have started adjusting the aperture and shutter speed with the joystick, press the shutter button halfway down until the camera beeps. The screen then shows a scale of tick marks ranging from -2 to +2 EV, with a zero at the mid-point and a little yellow indicator that moves along the scale. With this scale on the screen, you can adjust either aperture or shutter speed in turn until the yellow indicator settles over the zero point, indicating a standard exposure. Of course, you can adjust the settings however you want, leaving the indicator far to the right or left, as you please, possibly resulting in an over-exposed or underexposed image. But the camera is providing this display to show you what settings it would consider to yield a correct exposure given the existing lighting conditions. The scale stays on the screen for as long as you are making adjustments with the joystick, and for about ten seconds if you are not making adjustments. You can press the shutter button down to take the picture at any time.

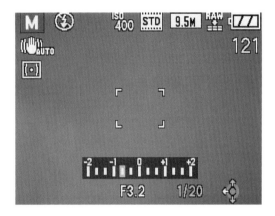

Scene Mode

Scene Mode is a rather different animal from the other shoot-ing modes we have discussed. This mode does not have a single defining feature, such as permitting control over one or more aspects of exposure. Instead, when you select Scene mode, and then choose a particular scene type within that mode, you are in effect telling the camera what sort of environment the pic-ture is being taken in and what kind of image you are looking for, and you're letting the camera make a group of decisions as to what settings to use to produce that result.

I did not use Scene Mode very much at first, though after us-ing it for a while I came to appreciate its usefulness, particu-larly in certain situations. Let's take a look at how it works and you can decide for yourself whether you might take advantage of it on some occasions.

You enter Scene mode by turning the Mode dial to the SCN indicator. Now, unless you want to settle for whatever type of scene setting is already in place, you now need to make an-other choice, and pick one from the fairly impressive list of possibilities.

To make this further choice, you need to use the menu system. When you select Scene mode, the menu system itself changes. Ordinarily, the menu system has only two main branches: Re-cord (or Playback, if you have the camera set to Play), and Setup. Now that you're in Scene mode, there is a third branch of the menu system, named Scene. It takes over as the first choice at the top of the menu system once you have pushed the Menu/Set button. (Actually, the Scene menu may appear immediately once you select the Scene mode with the Mode dial; that behavior is controlled through the Setup menu, as discussed later.)

Once the Scene menu is displayed, press the right cursor button, and the selector (a yellow outline) moves onto the first choice of Scenes, which is Portrait. One very good thing about the Scene menu system is that each scene type is labeled as you move the selector over it, so you are not left trying to puzzle out what each icon represents.

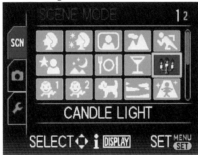

If you want a bit more information, press the Display button (the furthest button down on the camera's back, just to the right of the LCD screen) while in the Scene menu, and the display will give you a brief description of the Scene type that is shown in the menu.

Keep pushing the right button to move the selector over the other scene types; when you reach the screen's right edge, the selector moves down to the left item in the next row down. You also can use the other cursor buttons to navigate back and forth through the rows of scene types. You can speed through the Scene menu a full screen at a time by using the Zoom lever.

That's all there is to do to select a scene type. But there are numerous choices, and you need to know something about each choice to know whether it's one you would want to select. In general, each different scene type carries with it a variety of settings, including things like focus mode, flash status, range of shutter speeds, sensitivity to various colors, and others. Let's look at the complete list of scene types, so you can make an informed choice.

Portrait: For rich flesh tones. You are advised to stand fairly close to the subject and set the zoom to full telephoto, so as to blur the background if possible. The camera sets itself to Intelligent Exposure and initially sets the autofocus mode to Face Detection. The flash mode is initially set to Auto/Red-Eye Reduction.

Soft Skin: Similar to Portrait; detects flesh tones in faces and adds a "soft effect" to those areas. Intelligent Exposure is set. Flash mode is initially set to Auto/Red-Eye Reduction.

Self-Portrait: This Scene type is intended for you to take a photo of yourself, such as by holding the camera at arm's length and pointing back at you. The main trick the camera performs in this mode is that it lights up the self-timer lamp when you press the shutter button halfway, to show that the scene (that is, you) is in focus. (It does this because you aren't able to check the focus on the LCD screen.) If the lamp blinks, that means the scene is not in focus, so you need to make adjustments. The user's manual recommends that you set the self-timer for two seconds; the ten-second setting is not available. The camera automatically sets the zoom range to wide angle, which you should leave as is. The focus range will be from about 1 foot to 2.3 feet (30 cm to 70 cm). Intelligent Exposure is turned on, and the flash mode is initially set to Auto/ Red-Eye Reduction.

Scenery: This style is intended for photographs of landscapes and vistas in the distance. The autofocus range is set from about 16 feet to infinity. Intelligent Exposure is set. The flash is set to off.

(One interesting point about this scene type is that, even if you open up the flash unit, it will be automatically set to be forced off, and will not fire. Ordinarily, there is no way for the user to force the built-in flash off when the unit is open, but the camera can do so automatically when set to the Scenery style and a few others.)

Sports: This style is meant to stop the action of sports in bright daylight using fast shutter speeds at distances of 16 feet or more. The camera sets itself to use Intelligent Exposure and Intelligent ISO, with a minimum ISO set to 800. (I'll discuss all of the settings relating to ISO, or sensitivity to light, in Chapter 4. Briefly, with a higher-numbered ISO setting, the camera is more sensitive to light, and therefore can use a faster shutter speed. The tradeoff is the possibility of added "noise" or fuzziness of the image.) The flash can be used if you want to activate it.

Night Portrait: This style is designed for a portrait in low-light conditions, preferably with the camera on a tripod and possibly even using the self-timer or a cable release (see Appendix B) to avoid shaking the camera. It's recommended that you zoom the lens back to its wide angle setting and aim at a subject between about 4 and 16 feet (1.2 and 4.9 meters) from the camera; the optimum distance is about 5 feet (1.5 meters). If the flash is used, it will be set to slow sync red-eye reduction. The camera will be set to Intelligent Exposure. If possible, the subject should be asked not to move for about a second while the image is being exposed.

Night Scenery: This style is meant for night-time scenes with the camera on a tripod, and also using the self-timer or a cable release to minimize camera shake. The shutter speed will be set for an exposure as long as 8 seconds. Because this style is for scenery and not portraits, the focus range will be from 16 feet (4.9 meters) to infinity. The flash will be forced off, and will not fire.

Food: This style is for taking pictures of food. You may want to use this setting if you're participating in the recent trend to keep a photographic food diary, taking a picture of every meal before you eat it. Or you could use it to take pictures for your cookbook. In any event, the idea here is to take a fairly close-up picture without flash, though the flash will be available if you want to use it. The autofocus range will be the same as for autofocus macro, about two inches (5 cm) at wide angle, or two feet (61 cm) at telephoto, to infinity.

Party: This style is for taking pictures in lighted interior settings, such as wedding receptions and other social events. It's recommended to use a tripod, and you can use flash if you want to. The recommended distance for shooting is about five feet (1.5 meters).

Candle Light: The name is self-explanatory, but oddly enough, this scene type allows the flash to fire if you want it, which would seem to defeat the purpose. The manual does say it would be better if you didn't use flash, and I would think you would want to follow that advice. Focus range is the same as for autofocus macro, or about two inches (5 cm) at wide angle, or two feet (61 cm) at telephoto, to infinity.

Baby 1 and Baby 2: These two settings both are geared for taking baby pictures in the same way; the only reason there are two different settings is because you can enter the birth dates and names of two children into the camera, and have each child's name and age displayed along with the picture. The attraction here is that the camera will keep track of what age the child is in each photo.

When you select one of these settings, the camera will present you with a screen with options for name and age; you can leave either or both of these set to Off if you want, or enter the data. If you want to enter them, the camera gives you menus from which to choose year, month, day, and letters for the names.

Apart from the names and ages, the Baby 1 and Baby 2 scene styles set the camera to use a weaker-than-normal flash output, focus range the same as macro mode, Intelligent ISO (light sensitivity) activated, and ISO Limit (see later discussion) set to ISO 400.

Pet: The Pet scene style is similar to Baby 1 and Baby 2 in that you can set your pet's name and age. The initial setting for the Autofocus Assist lamp is Off. (The Autofocus Assist lamp and its setting are discussed in Chapter 5.) Intelligent ISO is activated, and ISO Limit is set to ISO 800.

Sunset: This scene style is designed to highlight the vivid reds of a sunset. The flash is forced off, and won't fire even if you open it up in dark conditions. It would be a good idea to use a tripod if possible, because the exposure time may be long enough that it would be difficult to hold the camera steady throughout the exposure. Note that, although you may often use this mode to take pictures including the setting sun, it also can be useful to take images, like the one below, at the time of sunset, but facing away from the sun, showing the effects of the sunset on other objects, like the trees in this picture.

High Sensitivity: With this type, the ISO is set high, in a range between ISO 1600 and ISO 6400, making it possible for the camera to expose the picture correctly at a faster shutter speed. The Quality setting is automatically placed at Standard and the Picture Size is set to 3 MP or less, depending on the aspect ratio setting, so the resulting pictures will not be suitable for big enlargements, possibly only 4 by 6 inch (10.2 by 15.2 cm) prints. The focus range is that of macro mode.

This scene type is suitable for reducing motion blur when shooting in low light, such as indoors. Obviously, you will be sacrificing quality if you use this style, so it's best used only if there are no other viable options, or if you want to achieve a particular effect by increasing the visual noise in the image. You should note that, as with some other features of the LX3 (such as Flash Burst), using this particular scene type is the only way you can make one particular setting. There is no way to set the ISO to 6400 other than setting the scene type to High Sensitivity; that value is not available through the normal ISO menu. So if you need to take pictures that may involve motion in a very dark area without flash, remember the High Sensitivity setting in Scene mode. The image on the next page was taken in High Sensitivity mode at ISO 6400 at night in an area that was lit only by light from an adjacent room.

Hi-Speed Burst: This scene type sets the camera to fire rapid bursts of shots when you hold down the shutter button. The camera will take pictures continuously at a rate of about 6 pictures per second, up to a total of about 35 pictures if you're using the built-in memory, and up to a maximum of 100 pictures if you're using an SD memory card. The camera automatically sets the Quality to Standard, which means you'll be able to make good prints only up to a size of about 4 by 6 inches (10.2 by 15.2 cm). The focus range is set to the macro focus range. Once the focus, zoom, exposure, white balance, and ISO level are set for the first picture, all of those settings stay locked in for the rest of the pictures in the burst. The camera sets the ISO to between 500 and 800 so the shutter can fire rapidly and still expose the picture adequately. Also, the Quality setting varies with the aspect ratio. For maximum quality (3 MP), choose 4:3 aspect ratio; for 2.5 MP, choose 3:2 or 1:1; for 2 MP, choose 16:9.

The Hi-Speed Burst setting is good to have in your bag of tricks if there's an occasion when you need to take a quick range of pictures of a changing scene, such as a breaking news event, when you need to get the camera set quickly and don't have time to search for the right settings to get rapid-fire shooting. Of course, the tradeoff in image quality is a factor you need to consider, but if something happens quickly and you need a rapid sequence of shots, this scene type is better than nothing.

Flash Burst: This scene type sets the camera to take a burst of five pictures as fast as possible when you hold down the shutter button, firing the flash each time. Apart from the firing of the flash and the more limited number of pictures taken, this style is similar to Hi-Speed Burst. In particular, the quality is limited according to the aspect ratio, and the initial settings for the first picture are locked in for the subsequent pictures. Intelligent ISO is activated with an ISO limit of 3200. Because of the need for the flash to recycle, the burst is not quite as fast as for Hi-Speed Burst, but it is still fairly rapid.

Starry Sky: This setting is designed for one purpose: for you to set the camera on a tripod and take a picture of the stars in the night sky. The flash is forced off, image stabilization is turned off (because the camera will be on a tripod), and the ISO is set to 100. When you first select this scene style, the camera presents you with a screen to navigate through with the up and down buttons, to select either 15, 30, or 60 seconds for the length of the exposure. You make that selection, and then press the shutter button to start the exposure. The camera counts the seconds down on the screen. After the exposure is finished, the camera counts down the same amount of time all over again, because it takes that long to process the photograph inside the camera. After the second countdown, the picture appears for viewing.

This is a good place to point out something that is true of this scene type in particular, and of other types as well. Don't let the name "Starry Sky" keep you from using this setting only for pictures of the night sky. It may be just what you need in any situation where a long exposure may yield good results. For example, I have used it to get interesting shots of houses lit up at night, like the image on the previous page. Starry Sky mode also could be used to capture trails of headlights and taillights from automobiles, and undoubtedly could be useful in many other situations.

Fireworks: This scene setting is used for fireworks displays. It's recommended to have the camera on a tripod. The camera sets the shutter speed to either 2 seconds or 1/4 of a second, depending on the setting of the image stabilization function. If stabilization is off, the camera chooses 2 seconds, presumably on the theory that the camera is on a tripod. If stabilization (discussed in Chapter 4) is on, the camera chooses 1/4 second, unless it has sensed that there is very little camera shake, indicating that a tripod is probably being used; in that case, the camera chooses 2 seconds. The ISO is set to 100.

Beach: This setting is designed to prevent the underexposure of subjects sitting on a beach, caused by the camera's being fooled by the brightness of the beach into closing down its aperture too much. The default setting for this scene style is to force the flash on to brighten the subject so it is not overwhelmed by the surrounding brightness.

Snow: This setting is designed, according to the user's manual, to let you take pictures of snow that show the snow to be "as white as possible." It's not clear exactly how this is accomplished, though the camera apparently boosts the gain slightly and produces a warmer than usual image.

Aerial Photo: This setting is designed for taking pictures through an airplane window, when it may be difficult to focus on a subject such as clouds. The instructions are to aim at something with high contrast, press the shutter button halfway to lock in the focus, and then take the picture.

Pin Hole: This Scene type is meant to simulate the look of a picture taken with a pin hole camera, a very rudimentary device that uses a small hole in a wall or other barrier instead of a lens, and typically produces a soft, somewhat cloudy and dark image, especially at the corners. The quality is set to Standard, and the focus range is set to the same as for macro focus. This setting yields pictures suitable for 4 by 6 inch (10.2 by 15.2 cm) prints.

It's worth noting that some photographers really love this setting, which is not offered by many cameras. The results certainly are not high-quality in terms of sharpness or resolution, but this scene type offers an interesting effect that cannot readily be achieved in other ways, unless you're quite handy with a computer editing program such as Photoshop.

Film Grain: This scene type is similar to Pin Hole, in that it purposely degrades the image to achieve an effect that may be considered artistic. In this case, the camera sets the quality to Standard and ISO to 1600, yielding a noisy, grainy effect, and produces a black-and-white image instead of color. Here, again, you could achieve a similar effect in Photoshop, but it's nice to have this option for in-camera processing of the image in an interesting way.

High Dynamic: This scene type was not included when the LX3 originally was released; this was the one type that was added in the upgrade to firmware version 2.0. With this setting, the camera boosts the dynamic range of the photograph by increasing the detail in shadowed areas without over-exposing the highlights. This option offers some of the qualities of High Dynamic Range (HDR) photography, though on a small scale. HDR is the practice of taking two or more shots of the same scene using different exposure settings, then combining those images in software that is designed to merge them to produce a final image that shows clear detail in both highlights and shadowed areas. When you select the High Dynamic scene type on the LX3, you have three sub-options to choose from, using the up and down cursor buttons: Standard, Art, and Black & White. The Art option produces a more dramatic effect of enhanced and contrasting colors. This scene type works only with JPEG images, not RAW files.

The three images shown below and on the following page illustrate the effects of this setting: The first picture was taken in Program Mode with no unusual settings; the second was taken in High Dynamic scene mode with the Standard setting; the last one was taken with High Dynamic set to Art.

Chapter 4
Advanced Topics

The Recording Menu

Much of the power of the LX3 resides in the many options provided in the Recording menu, which gives the user control over the appearance of the images and the ways in which they are captured. Depending on your own preferences, you may not have to use this menu too much. You may prefer to use the various scene types, which choose many of the options for you, or you may prefer, at least on occasion, to use Intelligent Auto mode, in which the camera makes its own choices. However, it's nice to know that you do have this degree of control over many functions available if you want it, and it is very useful to understand what types of items you can exercise control over.

The Recording menu is quite easy to use once you have played around with it a bit. As I discussed earlier, the menu options can change depending on the setting of the shooting Mode dial on top of the camera. For example, if you're in Intelligent Auto mode, the Recording menu options are very limited, because that mode is for a user who wants the camera to make almost all of the decisions without input from the photographer. For the following discussion, I'm assuming you have the camera set to Program mode (shooting Mode dial turned to the P setting), because in that setting you have access to all of the power of the Recording menu. (Note that some menu options will be unavailable in certain situations.)

So, put the camera into Recording mode with the Record-Playback slide switch at the top of the camera's back, and turn the Mode dial on top of the camera to P for Program mode. You enter the menu system by pressing the center button in the five-button array on the back of the camera—the one labeled Menu/Set.

Once you press the center button, you are initially in the Recording menu. If you wanted to get into the Setup menu, you would press the left button in the five-button array, and that would take you into the Setup menu system, symbolized by a wrench icon. For now, we're staying in the Recording menu.

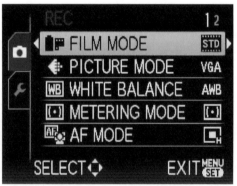

You'll see a fairly long list of options, each option occupying one line, with its name in capital letters, its icon on the left, and its current setting on the right. You have to scroll through several screens to see all of the options. If you find it tedious to scroll using the up and down cursor buttons, here's a tip for navigating any menu system: You can use the Zoom lever on top of the camera to speed through the menus one full screen at a time. Also, depending on the menu option, you may be able to reach it more quickly by reversing direction with the cursor buttons, and wrapping around to reach the option you want. (For example, if you're on the top line of the menu, you can scroll up to reach the bottom option.)

Some of the menu's lines may have a dimmed, "grayed-out" appearance, meaning they cannot be selected under the present settings. For example, if you have set the Quality to RAW, you cannot set the Picture Size, which is automatically set to the maximum of 10 MP when RAW is selected, so the Picture Size line is grayed out. Also, if you have set the Quality to RAW, you cannot set certain other functions, such as Intelligent Exposure, Digital Zoom, Audio Record, and Multi Aspect (taking multiple pictures bracketed with different aspect ratios). If you want to follow along with the discussion of all of the options on the Recording menu, you might want to set the Quality to Fine, which is the setting with the icon of an arrow pointing down onto two rows of bricks. To do that, scroll down using the bottom button until the Quality line is highlighted, then press the right button to pop up the submenu. Scroll up or down as needed to highlight the icon with the six bricks, and then press the Menu/Set button to select that option.

Okay, now you have access to every option on the Recording menu. We'll start at the top, and discuss each option on the way down the list.

Film Mode: This top option in the Recording menu gives you several options for setting the "Film" mode for the camera. Just as various physical films used in cameras have considerably different characteristics, these settings yield differing results for your images in terms of warmth, color cast, and other attributes.

There are a few points you need to bear in mind about these settings. First, they are not available in all recording modes.

They are available only when the shooting mode is set to Program, Aperture Priority, Shutter Priority, Manual, Custom, or Motion Picture. (There are limited Film Mode settings available in Motion Picture mode.) You cannot choose a Film Mode when you have set the camera to Intelligent Auto mode or any of the scene types; in those cases, the camera makes a choice for you.

There are four parameters that are varied for these settings: contrast, sharpness, color saturation, and noise reduction. Even though each of these film modes has basic settings of those four items, you can still make further adjustments and set the camera to memorize the new settings for each category. Use the up and down cursor buttons to scroll to any of the four parameters, then use the left and right buttons to change the value of that parameter up to two levels, either positive or negative. The camera will remember those settings even when it is turned off.

One important point to note here: If you want to change any of those four parameters (contrast, sharpness, color saturation, or noise reduction), you have to do it through the Film Mode settings. There is no way to change the settings for any of these four items directly.

Here's one point that's not mentioned in the user's manual,

though it makes sense if you think about it. When you set Film Mode to any of the non-color settings, such as Standard BW, Dynamic BW, or Smooth BW, and the Quality is set to RAW, the picture you take will show up as black-and-white on the camera's LCD screen, but, when you import the image file into software that reads RAW files, the image will show up in color. This makes sense because the RAW format allows you to manipulate the "raw" data seen by the camera's sensor, which includes the color information. You can convert these images back to black-and-white on your computer by moving the saturation slider to zero in your RAW software. (Or, in more recent versions of Photoshop, you can use the far superior method available with the menu command Image - Adjustments - Black & White.)

Following are summaries of each of the available Film Mode settings:

Standard: No change from the normal setting.

Dynamic: Increased saturation (intensity or vividness) and contrast of the colors in the image.

Nature: Brighter red, green, and blue.

Smooth: Lower contrast, for softer and clearer color.

Vibrant: Similar to Dynamic, but even greater increase in saturation and contrast.

Nostalgic: Decreased saturation and contrast, giving an antique or washed-out look.

Standard BW: Standard settings, but black-and-white image.

Dynamic BW: Contrast is increased for black-and-white image.

Smooth BW: Lower contrast to soften the picture; black and white.

My Film 1: User-generated settings. (See discussion below.)

My Film 2: Second set of user-generated settings.

Multi Film: Burst of up to three images using different film modes. (See discussion below.)

My Film 1 and 2: These two options are initially set to the Standard setting. You can adjust all four parameters (contrast, sharpness, saturation, and noise reduction) to whatever levels you want, to a total of plus or minus two levels from normal. The camera will remember those settings until you change them again, even after it has been turned off and then on again. When you play back a picture taken with either the My Film 1 or My Film 2 setting, the LCD screen will show STD for Standard, but the indicator will be in yellow instead of white, to show that the Standard setting was altered by the user. In other words, don't look for "My Film 1" or anything similar to appear on the playback screen for a picture taken with that setting; instead, the camera shows STD in yellow. In fact, whenever you have altered the settings of the four parameters, whether for a My Film setting or for one of the named Film Mode settings (Dynamic, Vibrant, etc.), the indicator for that setting shows up in yellow on the LCD screen when the picture is played back (if the display is set to show full details).

Multi Film: This setting, which is intended to let you take up to three images at different Film Mode settings with one press of the shutter button, needs a bit of explanation. One important point is that this setting does not work if you are shooting RAW images. You can set the camera to Multi Film for RAW images, but the camera will take only one image, not multiple ones. So if you want to take advantage of the Multi Film feature, set the Quality to Fine or Standard, but not to RAW, RAW plus Fine, or RAW plus Standard. (I suppose the theory here is that, if you're shooting in RAW mode, you can manipulate the colors and other qualities of the image with your software, so you don't really need to bracket your exposures in this way.)

Here's another point to be aware of. The user's manual at page 75 says you can set Multi Film to take multiple pictures "up to a maximum of three films." That's true, but what's also true is that it can only be set to take either two or three images. When you think about it, it would no longer be a "multi" film setting if you could set it to take just one picture. When you get into the settings, remember that you have to set at least two of the Multi Film slots to take pictures using one Film Mode or another; it's only the third slot in Multi Film that has an "Off" setting.

If you're following along with your camera, I suggest setting the Quality to Fine (the icon with the six bricks under an arrow). Get into the Film Mode settings through the Record menu by pressing the center button in the five-button array, then press the right button repeatedly until you reach the Multi Film setting. Using the down button, navigate to the top slot, called Multi Film1, then use the right arrow to set that slot to whatever Film Mode you want. (Note: If you have altered any of the Film Modes previously by changing their parameters, that mode will show up in yellow, so you'll know it is not set to the factory settings.) As discussed above, you have to set this slot and the next one to some Film Mode; you cannot turn it off. Repeat for slot 2, then go down to slot 3 and set it to a Film Mode or set it to Off if you want only two images taken, rather than all three. Press the center button enough times to exit completely from the menu system. Now the M Film indicator will appear at the top center of the LCD screen. When you press the shutter button, the camera will take two or three images at the Film Mode settings you selected.

Picture Size: This setting controls the number of megapixels (MP) in the images you record with the camera, up to and including its maximum of 10.1 MP. (The highest number shows up as simply 10 MP on the menu.)

The maximum MP setting is controlled by the aspect ratio that you have set. You can set the aspect ratio to one of three settings using the switch on top of the lens barrel: 4:3, 3:2, or 16:9. Using the menu system, you can set the aspect ratio to 1:1, for a square image. If you set the aspect ratio to 4:3, the maximum MP setting is the full 10 MP. If you set the aspect ratio to 3:2, the camera achieves that image shape by cutting off some MP vertically but adding some horizontally, so the maximum setting for Picture Size is 9.5 MP. At the 16:9 setting, even more vertical MP are lost but horizontal ones are added, and the maximum Picture Size is 9 MP. With the aspect ratio set to 1:1, the maximum picture size is 7.5 MP. Finally, if you want to set the Picture Size to its smallest, 0.3 MP, perhaps in order to maximize the number of images you can take, you have to set the aspect ratio to 4:3. At any of the other three aspect ratio settings, the minimum picture size is at least 2 MP.

There are several points that you need to bear in mind about the MP settings. First, the higher the MP setting, the better the overall quality of the image, all other factors being equal. However, you can create a fuzzy and low-quality image with a high MP setting with no trouble at all; the MP setting does not guarantee a great image. But if all other factors are equal, a higher MP count should yield noticeably higher image quality. Also, when you have a large MP count in your image, you have some leeway for cropping it; you can select a portion of the image to enlarge to the full size of your print, and still retain acceptable image quality.

On the other hand, images with high MP counts eat up your storage space more quickly than those with low MP counts. If you are running low on space on your SD card and still have a lot of images to capture, you may need to reduce your Picture Size setting so you can fit more images on the card.

Extended Optical Zoom

Another point to consider is how much zoom you need or want. You might not think that picture size is related to zoom, but with the LX3, it is. The camera has a feature called Extended Optical Zoom, designated as EZ in the illustrations in the user's manual. Here is how it works. When you set the Picture Size to 3 MP, for example, you will find that you can zoom in further than you can with the Picture Size set to its maximum. If you try this, you will see an EZ designation appear on the LCD screen to the left of the Zoom scale, as you move the zoom lever on top of the camera toward the T setting, for Telephoto. The scale will extend to a zoom level of 4.5X normal, rather than the ordinary maximum zoom of 2.5X.

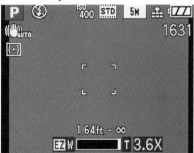

This feature needs further explanation. The lens of the LX3 has an actual, physical focal length range of 5.1 millimeters (mm) to 12.8 mm. At its full wide-angle (un-zoomed) setting, the lens's focal length is 5.1 mm. As with most digital cameras today, the camera's documentation converts this figure to the "35mm-equivalent," that is, to the focal length for the lens that would be the equivalent of this lens on a camera that uses 35mm film. In this case, that focal length is 24mm, which is still a very wide setting for a standard lens. The 35mm equivalent value for the zoomed setting of the LX3's lens is 60mm. So the 35mm equivalent zoom range for this lens is 24mm to 60mm.

Normally the maximum zoom value for the LX3's lens is 60mm, or 2.5 times the unzoomed setting of 24mm. However, when you set the Picture Size to a value lower than the maximum 10MP, such as 3MP, the camera lets you zoom in further on the subject you are viewing using the Zoom lever. What is actually happening is that the camera takes the normal area that the optical zoom "sees," and then blows it up to a larger size, which is possible because the lower MP setting means the camera is using a lower resolution and can present a larger zoomed image. Extended Optical Zoom has a maximum power of 4.5 times the normal lens's magnification.

To sum up the situation with Extended Optical Zoom, whenever you set the Picture Quality to a level below 9MP, you get a bit of additional zoom power because of the reduced resolution. In reality, you could achieve the same result by taking the picture at the normal zoom range with the Picture Quality set to the full 10MP or 9MP, and then cropping the image in your computer to enlarge just the part you want. But with Extended Optical Zoom, you do get the benefit of seeing a larger image on the LCD screen when you're composing the picture, and the benefit of having the camera perform its focus and exposure operations on the actual zoomed image that you want to capture, so the feature is not useless. You just need to decide whether it's of use to you in a particular situation.

Digital Zoom

One other note before we leave this subject: to add an extra dash of confusion, the LX3 has another feature called Digital Zoom. This feature is activated through the Recording menu by scrolling down through the various options until you reach Digital Zoom. You then push the right key to pop up the submenu, use the up or down key to select ON, and press the center button (Menu/Set) to activate the feature.

With Digital Zoom, unlike Extended Optical Zoom, you get what the user's manual calls "deterioration" of the image. As with all digital cameras, Digital Zoom is a way of further enlarging the pixels that are displayed so the image appears larger; there is no additional resolution available, so the image can quickly begin to appear blocky and of low quality. Experts often recommend staying away from this sort of zoom feature. As with Extended Optical Zoom, it might occasionally be of use to help you in viewing a distant subject. Digital Zoom has a maximum power of 4 times the normal lens's magnification. When you combine these two features, there is a maximum total zoom power of about 18 times normal. Digital Zoom is not available in Intelligent Auto mode. (EZ is available in that mode, because it is activated by setting the Picture Size, which is one of the few menu items available in iA mode.)

Quality

The next setting on the Recording menu is Quality. We have already discussed the Quality setting briefly, in connection with basic picture taking. I'll mention the main information again here, in order to provide a description of all of the features on the Recording menu.

It's important to distinguish the Quality setting from the Picture Size setting. As we discussed above, Picture Size concerns the image's resolution, or the number of megapixels in the image. Quality has to do with how the image's digital information is compressed for storage on the SD card and, later, on the computer's hard drive. There are three levels of quality available: RAW, Fine, and Standard. RAW is in a category by itself, and we'll spend some time in Chapter 8 discussing how to work with files of that type. Fine and Standard are two levels of compression for computer image files which use the JPEG standard. Images saved with Fine quality are subjected to less compression than those saved with Standard quality. In other words, Standard-quality images have their digital data "compressed" or "squeezed" down to a smaller size to allow more of the files to be stored on an SD card or computer drive, with a corresponding loss of image quality. The more compression an image is subjected to, the less clear detail it will contain. So unless you are running out of space on your storage medium, you probably want to leave the Quality setting at Fine to ensure the better quality. (Unless you have opted to shoot in the RAW format for maximum quality.)

With the LX3, besides choosing any one of the three individual Quality settings (RAW, Fine, or Standard), you also have the option of setting the camera to record images in RAW *plus* either Fine or Standard. If you choose that option, the camera will record each image in two files: one RAW, and the other a JPEG file in either Fine or Standard quality, depending on your selection. If you then play the image back in the camera, you will see only one image, but if you copy the files to your computer, you will find two image files; one with a .jpg extension and one with an .rw2 extension. The RAW file will be much larger than the JPEG one. In one example I just tried on my computer, the RAW file was about 12 MB and the JPEG file was about 4 MB.

Why would you choose the option of recording images in both RAW and JPEG formats at the same time? Say you're taking pictures of a one-time event such as a wedding or graduation; you may want to preserve them in RAW for the highest quality, but also have them available for quick review on a computer that might not have software that reads RAW files. Or you might want to quickly send the images to friends by e-mail. Having the images also recorded in JPEG format allows you to skip the step of translating the files from RAW to JPEG format, which most people can easily view on their computers. Here, again, this is an option that's open to you if space on your SD card is not a major consideration. If you have a high-capacity card, or multiple cards available, you may want to take advantage of the option of recording images in both RAW and JPEG formats at the same time.

Intelligent ISO

The next item on the Recording menu is Intelligent ISO. This setting has only two possible values - On or Off. If it is turned on, Intelligent ISO causes the camera to sense movement in the image, and, if necessary, to use its circuitry to set the ISO to a value that will allow the use of a fast enough shutter speed to minimize or avoid blurriness from motion.

This topic calls for some background discussion of ISO. These initials stand for International Standards Organization. When I first started in film photography several decades ago, this standard was called ASA, for American Standards Association. The ISO acronym reflects the more international nature of the modern photographic industry.

The original use of the ISO/ASA standard was to designate the "speed," or light sensitivity, of film. So, for example, a "slow" film might be rated ISO 64, or even ISO 25, meaning it takes a considerable amount of exposure to light to create a usable image on the film. Slow films yield higher-quality, less-grainy images than faster films. There are "fast" films available, some black-and-white and some color, with ISO ratings of 400 or even higher, that are designed to yield usable images in lower light. Such films can often be used indoors without flash, for example.

With digital technology, the industry has retained the ISO concept, but it applies not just to film, but to the light sensitivity of the camera's sensor, because there is no film involved in a digital camera. The ISO ratings for digital cameras are supposed to be essentially equivalent to the ISO ratings for films. So if your camera is set to ISO 100, there will have to be a good deal of light to expose the image properly, but if the camera is set to ISO 1600, a reasonably good (but "noisier" or "fuzzier") image can be made in very low light.

The upshot of all of this is that, in general, you want to shoot your images with the camera set to the lowest ISO possible that will allow the image to be exposed properly. (One exception to this rule is if you want, for creative purposes, the grainy look that comes from shooting at a high ISO value.) For example, if you are shooting indoors in low light, you may need to set the ISO to a high value (say, ISO 800) so you can expose the image with a reasonably fast shutter speed. If the camera were set to a lower ISO, it would need to use a slower shutter speed to take in enough light for a proper exposure, and the resulting image would likely be blurry and possibly unusable.

To summarize: Shoot with low ISO settings (around 100) when possible; shoot with high ISO settings (say 400 or higher, up to

1600 or even 3200) when necessary in dimmer light to allow a fast shutter speed to stop action and avoid blurriness, or when desired to achieve a creative effect with graininess.

With that background, let's look at what the Intelligent ISO setting can be useful for. When you turn this feature on through the Recording menu, the camera sets the ISO automatically to a level that allows the use of a shutter speed to avoid blurriness from camera shake. Presumably, this would be in the range of 1/30 of a second or faster. The ISO range available for this setting is limited by another setting that you can make — the ISO LIMIT setting. That setting, which is two lines further down on the Recording menu, lets you set the upper limit for the ISO to 200, 400, 800, 1600, 3200, or AUTO. So if you set the ISO Limit to 400 and Intelligent ISO to On, the camera will choose an ISO setting up to 400 to avoid camera shake. If you set the ISO Limit to Auto, the upper limit will be 800, depending on the brightness of the scene.

Intelligent ISO is turned on automatically if the camera is set to Intelligent Auto mode or to any of these scene types: Sports, Baby, or Pet. Intelligent ISO is not available for the user to set when the camera is set to any of these Recording modes: Shutter Priority, Manual, or Scene. Intelligent ISO is also not available in Motion Picture recording mode.

Sensitivity

The next setting on the Recording menu is Sensitivity, which lets you set the ISO to a specific value. The possible values are 80, 100, 200, 400, 800, 1600, 3200, and Auto. When you set Sensitivity to Auto, the camera automatically adjusts the ISO to an appropriate setting up to the maximum value set with ISO Limit, if any has been set. When you set a numerical value for Sensitivity, you cannot then set ISO Limit. If you have set

Intelligent ISO to ON, you cannot then set Sensitivity.

When would you want to use the Sensitivity setting? One example is if you want to achieve the highest-possible quality in your image, and you don't have to worry about camera movement, either because you are using a tripod so a slow shutter speed won't result in blur, or there is plenty of light so you will have a fast shutter speed. Then you could set the ISO to its lowest possible setting of 80 to achieve high quality. On the other hand, if you definitely want a grainy, noisy look, you can set the Sensitivity to 1600 or even 3200 to introduce noise into the image. You also might want a high ISO setting in order to use a fast shutter speed in low light.

One feature of the LX3 is that the camera can actually set the ISO as high as 6400, although you don't have access to that setting directly. In order to achieve that setting, you have to use the High Sensitivity Scene type, discussed in Chapter 3.

White Balance

This topic needs a bit of background discussion for those users who are new to digital photography. One issue that comes up in all photography is that film, or a digital camera's sensor, reacts differently to colors than the human eye does. When you or I see a scene in daylight or indoors under various types of artificial lighting, we generally do not notice a difference in the hues of the things we see depending on the light source. However, the camera's film or sensor does not have this auto-correcting ability. The camera "sees" colors differently depending on the "color temperature" of the light that illuminates the object or scene in question.

The color temperature of light is a numerical value that is expressed in a unit known as kelvins (K). A light source with a lower kelvin rating produces a "warmer" or more reddish light. A light source with a higher kelvin rating produces a "cooler" or more bluish light. For example, candlelight is rated at about 1,800 K; indoor tungsten light (such as from an ordinary light bulb) is rated at about 3,000 K; outdoor sunlight and electronic flash are rated at about 5,500 K; and outdoor shade is rated at about 7,000 K.

What does this mean in practice? If you are using a film camera, you may need a colored filter in front of the lens to "correct" for the color temperature of the light source. Any given color film is rated to expose colors correctly at a particular color temperature (or, to put it another way, with a particular light source). So if you are using color film rated for daylight use, you can use it outdoors without a filter. But if you happen to be using that film indoors, you will need a color filter to correct the color temperature; otherwise, the resulting picture will look excessively reddish because of the imbalance between the film and the color temperature of the light source.

With a modern digital camera, you do not need to worry about filters, because the camera can adjust its electronic circuitry to correct the "white balance," which is the term used in the context of digital photography for balancing color temperature.

The LX3, like many digital cameras, has a setting for Auto White Balance, which causes the camera to choose the proper color correction to account for any given light source. You get access to this setting through the Recording menu. Once you reach the White Balance line, press the right key to pop up the sub-menu.

You then have the following choices for the White Balance setting, most of them represented by icons: Auto White Balance (AWB); Outdoors, clear sky (sun icon); Outdoors, cloudy sky (cloud); Outdoors, shade (building); Flash only (lightning bolt with WB); Incandescent light (light bulb); Preset white balance 1 (number 1); Preset white balance 2 (number 2); Preset color temperature (the word "Set" with the letter K).

Most of the above settings are self-explanatory. You may want to experiment, though, and see if the named settings (outdoor sun, outdoor shade, etc.) produce the results you want. If not, you'll be better off setting the white balance manually.

To set white balance manually, select the White Balance option in the Recording menu, then press the right key to pop up the sub-menu and scroll to select Preset number 1 or 2. Then press the right key, and a rectangle will appear in the middle of the LCD screen. Aim the camera at a sheet of white paper under the light source you will be using, and fill the rectangle with the image of the white paper. Then press the center button to lock in that white balance setting. Now, until you change that setting, whenever you select that Preset (1 or 2, as the case may be), it will be set for the white balance you have just set. This system can be very useful if you often use a particular light source, and want to have the camera set to the appropriate white balance for that source.

If you want to set the color temperature directly by number, choose the Set K option from the White Balance menu. Then press the right key to pop up a screen with the value 2500K showing. You then can use the up and down arrows to adjust that value, anywhere from 2,500K up to 10,000K in increments of 100K.

But wait—there's one more level we can take this white balance adjustment to. If you really want to tweak the white balance setting to the nth degree, after you have selected your desired white balance setting and made any further selections, such as the numerical color temperature, or setting the balance with a white sheet of paper, before pressing the center button, press the right button one more time, and you will be presented with a screen for fine adjustments. You will see a pair of axes that intersect at a zero point, marked by a yellow dot. The four ends of the axes are labeled G, B, M, and A, for Green, Blue, Magenta, and Amber.

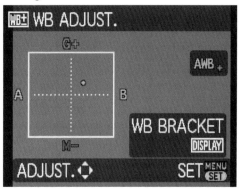

You can now use the four directional buttons to move the yellow dot away from the center toward any of the axes, to adjust these four values until you have the color balance exactly how you want it. The camera will remember this value whenever you select the white balance setting that you fine-tuned. A little green or magenta indicator shows up on the LCD screen beside the white balance icon when you have fine-tuned the setting towards green or magenta using the adjustment axes. The icon itself changes color to indicate adjustments towards blue or yellow.

White Balance Bracketing

There is still one more aspesct of white balance that needs to be discussed. Later on, I'll discuss exposure bracketing, also known as Auto Bracket, a feature by which the LX3 automatically takes three pictures at varying exposure settings, so you can have three options to choose from. You can do something similar with white balance -- set the camera to take three images at once with different white balances, to give you a better chance of having one image with the perfect color balance. I'm discussing this option here rather than in the section on Auto Bracket, because this option is accessed from the white balance setting screen.

Here is how to set up white balance bracketing. In the Recording menu, select white balance, then select a main setting, such as Daylight or Incandescent. Press the right button to access the fine adjustment screen, then press Display to activate white balance bracketing. You can then use the cursor buttons to set up an interval for the three images to be taken. When you press the buttons you will see three small, yellow dots appear on the horizontal or vertical axis, indicating the interval on the green to magenta or blue to yellow axis. Press the Menu/Set button twice to lock in the settings and exit the menu system. You will see the white balance bracketing icon on the LCD screen. Press the shutter release, and three images will be recorded with one shutter actuation, with slight variations in the white balance, according to your settings. This function does not work with RAW images, and does not work in Intelligent Auto or Motion Picture mode.

One final note about white balance: If you're shooting in RAW Quality, you don't have to worry about white balance at all, because, once you import the RAW file into your software, you can change the white balance however you want. This is one of the marvels of RAW. If you had the camera's white balance setting at Tungsten while shooting under a bright sun, you can just change the white balance setting to daylight in the RAW software, and no one need ever know about the error of your shooting.

Metering Modes

The next option on the Recording menu lets you choose what method the camera uses to meter the light and determine the proper exposure. The LX3 gives you your choice of three methods: Multiple, Center-weighted, and Spot. If you choose Multiple, the camera evaluates the brightness at multiple areas in the image that is shown on the LCD screen, and calculates an exposure that takes into account all of the various values. With Center-weighted, the camera gives greater emphasis to the brightness of the subject(s) in the center of the screen, while still taking into account the brightness of other areas in the image. With Spot, the camera evaluates only the brightness of the subject(s) in the small spot-metering area.

The user's manual recommends using the Multiple mode, presumably on the theory that that mode produces a reasonable choice for exposure, based on evaluating the overall brightness of everything seen on the LCD screen. However, if you want to make sure that one particular item in the scene is properly exposed, you may want to use the Spot method, and aim the spot metering area at that object or person, then lock in the exposure.

Choosing your metering method is less complicated than some other choices. Just enter the Recording menu and scroll down to the line for Metering Mode, then press the right arrow to activate the sub-menu with the three choices. The first icon, a rectangle with a pair of parentheses and a dot inside, represents Multiple mode; the second, a rectangle with a pair of parentheses inside, represents Center-weighted; and the third, a rectangle with just a dot inside, represents Spot.

If you select Multiple or Center-weighted, the metering process is quite straightforward; point the camera at the subject(s) you want and let the camera compute the exposure. If you choose Spot as your metering technique, the process can be more involved. Presumably, you will have a fairly small area in mind as the most important area for having the correct exposure; perhaps it is a small object you are photographing for an online auction. The LCD screen will display a small + in the center of the focusing brackets, and you need to be sure that + is touching the most important object. If that object is not in the center of the screen, then you may need to use the AE Lock control. That control is operated by the small button to the right of the joystick on the back of the camera. If you want that button to lock only the exposure, you can set that limitation through the Recording menu, down on the AF/AE Lock line. Just select AE Lock. Of course, the chances are pretty good that if you want to expose one object correctly you will also want to focus on that object, so it's often going to be okay to leave the lock button set to lock both autofocus and auto-exposure.

In any event, aim the camera so the + in the middle of the screen touches the object to be exposed correctly, then press the AE Lock button. The LCD screen will indicate that AE-L has been engaged. You can now move the camera back to compose the picture as you want it, perhaps with the correctly exposed object off to one side. You will notice that the exposure setting does not change as you re-compose the image. Press the shutter button, and the image is exposed as you wanted it.

The AE-Lock stays in effect until you cancel it by pressing the AE-Lock button again or turning off the camera.

Note that there is a sparsely-documented feature of the camera that lets you move the little + around the camera's screen so that you can place it right over the area of the picture that you want properly exposed. This will work only if, in addition to using the Spot metering mode, you are also using the Spot autofocus method. In that case, whenever you move the focusing target (see discussion below), the Spot-metering target moves along with it, so the target serves two purposes at once.

Some more notes on Metering Mode: This setting is not available in the Intelligent Auto or Scene modes. The LCD screen indicates which metering mode is active through an icon near the top left of the screen, below the recording mode and image stabilization icons. When Multiple metering is selected and the autofocus mode is set to Face Detection, the camera will attempt to expose a person's face correctly, assuming a face has been detected.

Autofocus Modes

This setting on the Recording menu lets you select among five different autofocus methods: Face Detection, AF Tracking, Multi-area, 1-area High-Speed, 1-area, and Spot. Here is how they work:

Face Detection: When you select this setting, the camera does not display any focusing brackets or rectangles until it detects a human face. If it does, it outlines the general area of the face with a yellow rectangle. Then, when you press the shutter button halfway down, the rectangle turns green when the camera has focused on the face. If the camera detects more than one face, it displays white rectangles. Any faces that are the same distance away from the camera as the face within the yellow rectangle will also be in focus, but the focus will be controlled by the face in the yellow rectangle.

As you might expect, Face Detection is not a perfect system. If conditions do not permit the camera to properly detect a face or faces, it is best to switch to another autofocus mode to avoid confusion. Face Detection cannot be set in Motion Picture mode or in the following varieties of Scene mode: Night Scenery, Food, Starry Sky, and Aerial Photo. Face Detection is automatically activated in Intelligent Auto mode. It is the initial setting for the following Scene types: Portrait, Soft Skin, Self Portrait, Night Portrait, Party, Candle Light, and Baby.

AF Tracking: This next setting for AF Mode allows the camera to maintain its focus on a moving subject. As with other AF modes, set this one using the Recording menu; scroll down to AF Mode and then select the second icon, which is a group of offset focus frames, designed to look like a moving focus frame. With this mode set, place the camera's focus frame on the moving subject and press the AF/AE Lock button, to the right of the joystick on the back of the camera. The camera will then do its best to keep the moving target in focus. It will display yellow brackets that should stay close to the subject on the LCD screen. When you are ready, press the shutter button to take the picture.

If the camera is not able to maintain focus on the moving subject, the focus frame will turn red and then disappear. AF Tracking cannot be set in Motion Picture mode, or in the following Scene mode types: Starry Sky, Fireworks, Pin Hole, or Film Grain.

When would you use AF Tracking? The idea here is to reduce the time it takes for you to be able to take a picture of a mov-

106

ing subject. If you are trying to snap a picture of your restless four-year-old, AF Tracking can give you a head start, so the camera's focus is close to being correct, and the focusing mechanism has less to do to achieve correct focus when you suddenly see the perfect moment to press the shutter button.

Multi-area: This method of focusing causes the camera to focus on up to five smaller focus areas within the overall autofocus area. You cannot select just any five small rectangles; the camera offers you several choices of groups of rectangles: the default choice is like a cross, with three rectangles across and three rectangles down, intersecting on the center rectangle. The other choices are five rectangles straight across the middle of the screen; four rectangles at the right or left side of the screen in a sideways T shape; or three rectangles across, toward the top or bottom of the screen.

You make these selections in one of two ways. If you have just scrolled to AF Mode on the menu, you can press the right key while the Multi-area mode selection is highlighted, to move directly to setting the autofocus areas. Or, if you are not in the menu system, you can press the Focus button on the top right of the camera, and then use the cursor buttons to move the selections as you wish. Then press the center button to make the selection. If you want to move the focus area back to the default selection in the middle of the screen, press the Focus button to return control to the focus brackets, then press the Display button at the bottom left of the area with buttons on the back of the camera. The focus area will also move back to its starting position when the camera is either switched to Intelligent Auto mode, enters Power-Save mode, or is turned off.

When you use the Multi-area focusing method, once you push the shutter button down halfway, the camera will display green rectangles to show you which of the multiple focus areas it has selected to focus on.

The Multi-area method can be useful if your subject is not in the center of the screen and you don't want to fool with moving the focus point around. With this method, the camera provides a fairly broad range of focus areas, and, if it finds a subject to focus on within the area that has been defined for it, it establishes the focus on that subject.

1-area High Speed: This method causes the camera to focus quickly on the center area of the screen. The camera uses a single, small focusing rectangle that you can move around the screen as you wish, using either of the methods discussed earlier in this chapter (right key then other cursor keys if you're already in the menu system; Focus button then cursor keys otherwise.) You can reset the rectangle back to the center of the screen using the same operations discussed above (Display button; switch to Intelligent Auto mode; Power-Save; or camera off).

The 1-area High Speed method is a very good one to use for general shooting, because it lets you quickly move the focus area to just where you want it. I prefer using this method to having to deal with multiple focusing rectangles.

1-area: This method is the same as 1-area High Speed without the high speed. The camera focuses on a small rectangle in the center of the screen; you can move the rectangle around as discussed above. You may ask what the advantage would be of using this focusing mode, when the 1-area high speed mode, discussed above, does the same thing, only faster. In my experience, in most cases there is no advantage to using this focusing method. Theoretically, it uses the extra time it takes to fine-tune the focus more precisely than the 1-area high speed mode. However, because this camera has a relatively wide depth of field, small differences in focus adjustment usually won't be noticeable in the final image. So you probably will do well if you stick with the 1-area high speed method.

Spot: This method is the same as 1-area, except that the focusing area is a very small one, considerably smaller than the rectangle used in the other methods. This method works well if you need to focus on a small subject, or a specific part of a subject. And, as was mentioned above in the discussion of the Spot-metering method, if you choose the Spot autofocus technique, you get a bonus: if you are using Spot-metering as well, whenever you move the focusing target, you are also moving the exposure target, so you can select a single, small area for your focus and exposure at the same time.

Pre AF

This next function on the Recording menu has three possible settings: Off, Q-AF, for Quick Autofocus, and C-AF, for Continuous Autofocus. They are set in the normal way, scrolling down to the line for Pre AF, then using the right key to pop up the sub-menu. If you set the camera to Q-AF, the camera will focus on the subject whenever the camera has settled down and is quite still, with only minor movement or shake. You do not need to press the shutter button halfway down to achieve focus; the camera focuses on its own. If you select C-AF, the camera focuses continuously without your pressing the shutter button halfway down, and does not wait for movement to settle down.

The advantage of these modes is that you will achieve a slight improvement in focusing time, because the camera does not wait until you press the shutter button to start the focusing process. The disadvantage is that the battery will be depleted faster than usual, especially in C-AF mode. So unless you believe that a split second for focusing time is critical, I would stay away from these settings.

AF/AE Lock

I talked about this control briefly in connection with Metering mode. This setting, accessed through the Recording menu, lets you change the function of the AF/AE Lock button, which is located to the right of the joystick on the back of the camera. You can set the button to lock both autofocus and auto-exposure settings, or just one or the other. The camera will indicate on the display, just below the image stabilization icon, which of the two values are locked, once you press the AF/AE Lock button and the values are locked in. It is not possible to lock exposure using the AF/AE button in Manual shooting mode, even though the display will still show the AE indicator if the button is set to lock exposure.

Intelligent Exposure

The I.Exposure, or Intelligent Exposure, setting causes the camera to adjust the exposure automatically to compensate for a situation in which there is a large difference in brightness between the background and the subject of the picture, as in the image below, taken facing into the sun.

It is not available when the Quality is set to RAW, so you need to set Quality to Standard or Fine to use this feature. It also is not available in Intelligent Auto or Scene modes. This feature can be set to Off, Low, or High, depending on how dramatic an effect you wish to achieve. When it is turned on to either level, its icon (an i with a dark and white circle) appears on the screen in black and white. When the feature is actually being triggered by the lighting conditions, the icon turns yellow.

The function of this option is to boost the ISO setting slightly, in the shadowed areas of the image only, when there is so much contrast in the scene as to cause the loss of details in shadows. The ISO will be raised enough to bring out more details in the shadowed areas. Its particular value lies in the fact that it can selectively alter the ISO setting for only the part of the image where that alteration is called for. This setting may override settings of ISO 80 or 100 and raise them somewhat.

Multiple Exposure

This function is more in the category of trick or creative photography than control of normal image-making. In a nutshell, it lets you create double or triple exposures in the camera. The steps to take are a bit unusual, because you actually carry out the picture-taking while in the Recording menu system.

Enter the Recording menu and scroll down to Multi. Expo, then press the right button, which takes you to a screen with the word Start highlighted. Press the center button (Menu/Set) to select Start. The screen then has the word End displayed; you can press the center button to end the process if you have had second thoughts.

If you are going to proceed, then compose and take the first picture. At this point the screen will display the image you just took along with the choices Next, Retake, and Exit. If you're not satisfied with the first image, scroll to Retake and select that option with the center button, then retake the first image. If you're ready to proceed to taking a superimposed image, leave Next highlighted and press the shutter button halfway down. This action produces the interesting effect of leaving the first image on the screen and making the screen live at the same time to take a new image. Compose the second shot as you want it, while viewing the first one, then press the shutter button fully to record that image. You can then repeat this process to add a third image, retake the second image, or exit the whole process. When you are done, you will have a single image that combines the two or three superimposed images you recorded.

Before you take the images using the Multi. Expo procedure, the menu gives you the option of setting Auto Gain on or off. If you leave it on, the camera adjusts the exposure based on the number of pictures taken; if you turn it off, the camera adjusts the exposure for the final superimposed image.

Digital Zoom

I discussed the digital zoom feature to some extent earlier in this chapter, in connection with the discussions of Picture Size and Extended Optical Zoom. Before we discuss the feature's use again, note a few restrictions: Digital Zoom is not available if you have the camera set to Intelligent Auto mode or if you have Intelligent ISO turned on. Also, it is not available if you have Quality set to RAW.

To recap its use briefly, you access Digital Zoom through the Recording Menu and turn it either on or off. Remember, this is really an artificial sort of zoom that does not give you any added "real" magnification; it just enlarges the existing image, making it fuzzy and blocky if you use too much of it. It's best avoided, except possibly for helping you view a distant object while composing your shot.

1:1 Aspect

As I noted earlier, with the upgrade to firmware version 2.0, Panasonic added a fourth aspect ratio of 1:1, yielding a square image for those who would like to have this option available for composing completely symmetical images in the camera. You can always crop your image to any aspect ratio in your editing software, but you may prefer to see the image in its square format while composing the shot in the camera. To activate this choice, set 1:1 Aspect either on or off with this menu selection.

Because this option was added through a firmware upgrade, you need to be aware of one issue stemming from the fact that other aspect ratios are set with the Aspect Ratio switch, while this one is set through the Recording menu: If you select 1:1 Aspect through the menu but then select any aspect ratio with the switch, the setting on the switch will take control. Also note that the 1:1 Aspect setting is not available in Intelligent Auto mode or Motion Picture mode.

113

Stabilizer

The LX3 is equipped with an optical image stabilization system, which works to minimize the effect of camera shake on the image when you're holding the camera in your hands rather than using it on a tripod or other support. There are four available settings: Off, Auto, Mode1, and Mode2. With Auto, the camera's circuitry determines the best mode to use, depending on conditions. With Mode1, the camera continuously compensates for camera shake while in Recording mode. With Mode2, the camera does not compensate for shake until the shutter button is pressed.

The camera automatically sets the stabilization to Mode2 in the Self Portrait style of Scene mode, and automatically turns all stabilization off in Starry Sky mode (because you'll be using a tripod). Stabilization cannot be turned off in Intelligent Auto mode. It cannot be set to Auto or Mode2 in Motion Picture mode. The status of the stabilization setting is displayed by an icon of a hand surrounded by wavy lines on the upper left of the LCD screen; the mode is indicated by the indicator Auto, 1, 2, or Off.

You get access to the Stabilizer menu through the Recording menu, in the normal way, pressing the right key to pop up the sub-menu with the four options for stabilization. The main consideration for whether to choose Mode1 or Mode2 is that Mode1 will use up the battery faster, because it continuously counters any camera shake, whereas Mode2 waits until the shutter button is pressed. As should be obvious, neither mode will do much good if there is a strong amount of camera shake present, or if you are operating under conditions that magnify camera movement, such as a long focal length, with no tripod and a slow shutter speed.

Personally, I leave the setting at Auto, which causes the camera to use Mode1 when zoomed in to telephoto and Mode2 when zoomed out to wide-angle. This setting makes sense, because there is more likely to be noticeable camera shake at the telephoto focal length, and it can be helpful to see the effects of stabilization on the LCD screen while you're composing the image in that situation. At the wide-angle setting, stabilization is not so much of an issue, and it is probably preferable to preserve battery life by leaving the stabilization to take place when the shutter button is pressed.

Minimum Shutter Speed

The setting for Minimum Shutter Speed lets you set the slowest shutter speed the camera will use, in a range from 1/250 second to one full second. You can use this setting when you want to avoid the camera shake that is likely to result from a slow shutter speed, such as 1/4 second. When you select any setting other than the default, which is 1/8 second, the camera displays the indicator MIN along with the minimum shutter speed in the lower right corner of the LCD screen. If the camera cannot achieve a proper exposure using this setting, the MIN indicator flashes in red when you press the shutter button halfway, meaning there is not enough light available. The camera will still take the picture if you continue to press the shutter button fully down; it has warned you, but will follow your instructions. In effect, this setting is a low-light alarm that you can ignore if you want to.

Note that this setting only has any effect when you are shooting in Program mode, either by setting the Mode dial to P, or by setting it to C1 or C2, with a custom setting that includes Program mode. This makes sense, because there are likely to be times when you would be hampered by having a minimum shutter speed of one second, the slowest available with this set-

115

ting. For example, if you're taking a long exposure in a dark area, or shooting infrared photos (see Chapter 8), you may need an exposure of several seconds. If you're in a situation like that, you have to remember not to set the camera to Program mode. You can choose Aperture Priority, Shutter Priority, Manual, or Scene mode. Note, though, that in Aperture Priority or Shutter Priority mode, the slowest shutter speed available is 8 seconds, whereas you can set it to a full 60 seconds in Manual mode. Also, as discussed earlier, some of the Scene types include long exposure times.

Audio Recording

The next option on the Recording Menu is Audio Recording. This function can be set only to On or Off. If you set it to On, when you take a picture an icon of a microphone appears on the screen. The camera will record audio for about five seconds, until the icon disappears, using the camera's built-in microphone, which is a tiny opening just in front of the Mode dial on top of the camera. When you play back a picture that has an audio recording attached, the screen tells you to press the up button to play the audio. You cannot control the volume of this audio during playback. However, you can control its volume to some extent by changing the general Volume setting in the Setup menu, discussed in Chapter 7. There is no other way to play the audio back, such as by saving it to your computer and using an audio-editing program to alter it or play it.

This function evidently is intended to let you make quick audio notes about the context of a picture, such as who the subject is, where the location is, and the like. I find the five-second limit to be confining. My audio memos often are cut off because I keep talking beyond the five-second limit. Note that you cannot turn on Audio Recording when the Quality setting is RAW and you cannot turn it on in Intelligent Auto mode. You can use it in the Scene modes and other shooting contexts. You cannot play back an audio recording from the Quick Review function; you have to be in Playback mode (using the Record-Playback switch) to play audio recordings.

I'm not a great believer in the need for audio memos, but if you feel it is important to attach an audio file to an image, you can record and attach a ten-second audio memo if you record it after the fact, using the Audio Dub function through the Playback Menu. (See Chapter 6 for a discussion of that option.)

Autofocus Assist Lamp

The AF Assist lamp is a reddish light source that is located on the front of the camera's body, near the top of the lens below the hot shoe and the Mode dial. (The hot shoe is the square bracket that accepts an external flash. It's called "hot" because it includes electrical connections that let it communicate with a flash that contains compatible circuitry.)

This lamp illuminates during focusing when the surrounding lighting is dim, to help the autofocus mechanism achieve the proper focus by providing enough light to define the shape of the subject. Ordinarily, this option is left turned on for normal shooting, because the light only activates when it is needed because of low-light conditions. However, you have the option of setting it to the off position so that it will never turn on. You might want to do this if you are trying to shoot your pictures without being detected, or without disturbing a subject such as a sleeping animal.

In Intelligent Auto mode, you cannot turn off the AF Assist lamp. In some of the Scene types, such as Starry Night and Fireworks, its default setting is Off, but you can go into the Recording menu system and turn it on if you wish. The lamp does not illuminate when you are using manual focus (unless you press the Focus button to give you an autofocus assist during the manual focusing process).

Flash Synchro

This setting is one you may not have a lot of use for, unless you encounter the particular situation it is designed for. Flash Synchro has two settings—1st and 2nd. Although the user's manual does not use this terminology, the 1st and 2nd are references to 1st-curtain sync and 2nd-curtain (also known as rear-curtain) sync. The normal setting is 1st, which causes the flash to fire early in the process when the shutter opens to expose the image. If you set it to 2nd, the flash fires later, just before the shutter closes.

The reason for having the 2nd-curtain sync setting available is to avoid having a strange-looking result in some unusual situations. This issue arises when you are taking a relatively long exposure, say one second, of a subject with taillights, such as a car or motorcycle at night, that is moving across your field of view. With 1st-curtain sync, the flash will fire early in the process, freezing the vehicle in a clear image. However, as the shutter remains open while the vehicle keeps going, the camera will capture the moving taillights in a stream that appears to be extending in front of the vehicle. If, instead, you use 2nd-curtain sync, the initial part of the exposure will capture the lights in a trail that appears behind the vehicle, while the vehicle itself is not frozen by the flash until later in the exposure. Therefore, with 2nd-curtain sync in this particular situation, the final image is likely to look more natural than with 1st-curtain sync.

To sum up the situation with 1st and 2nd Flash Synchro settings, a good general rule is to always use the 1st setting unless you are sure you have a real need for the 2nd setting. Using the 2nd setting makes it harder to compose and set up the shot, because you have to anticipate where the main subject will be when the flash finally fires late in the exposure process.

When you use the 2nd setting, the notation "2nd" appears next to the flash icon on the LCD screen when the flash is on.

The Flash Synchro setting is not available in Intelligent Auto mode, Motion Picture mode, or with any of the Scene types.

Red-Eye Removal

This menu option can be set either On or Off. When it is set on, and the camera is set to use flash with red-eye reduction, this function provides additional processing to digitally remove any redness that is detected near the eyes of a person. This function is automatically turned on in Intelligent Auto shooting mode.

External Viewfinder

This function can be set to either Off or On, depending on whether or not you have an external viewfinder attached to the camera. The LX3, like many compact digital cameras (as opposed to DSLRs), does not have a built-in viewfinder. Instead, it requires you to rely exclusively on its LCD screen to compose pictures. This system works quite well in normal light conditions, but in bright outdoor light or very dim light it can become difficult to see the screen. In addition, some photographers like to be able to hold the camera up to their eye rather than hold it out to see the LCD screen. Therefore, as I will discuss in the section on accessories (Appendix B), Panasonic offers an optional external viewfinder that attaches to the camera's hot shoe and lets you compose photographs without the use of the LCD screen. If you attach an external viewfinder (from Panasonic or another maker), you may want to turn off the LCD display to conserve battery power.

The On setting of this Recording menu option lets you turn the LCD screen off. Actually, it adds the turned-off-screen option to the cycle of options you get when you press the Display button on the bottom left of the control section on the back of the camera. With Ext. Viewfinder set to On, pressing the Display button in Recording mode cycles through the following options: full display information; focus brackets only; focus brackets and gridlines; display off. With Ext. Viewfinder set to Off, you get the same options, minus the display off option. When the display is turned off through this setting, the little green status light below the joystick on the camera's back lights up, presumably to let you know that the display is off by choice, and that the camera is still powered up and functioning.

Clock Set

The final option on the LX3's Recording menu is Clock Set, which functions in the same way as the same item on the Set-up menu. This option is also included here in the Recording menu, presumably for convenience in case you find that the time and date settings need to be adjusted.

120

Chapter 5
Advanced Topics — Other Controls

Not all of the settings that affect the recording process are located in the Recording menu. Several important functions are controlled by physical buttons and switches on the camera. We have already discussed some of these, but in order to make sure all of the information about these controls is included in one place, we'll go through each physical control, some in greater detail than others.

Aspect Ratio Switch

This switch, located on top of the lens barrel, has three possible settings: 4:3, 3:2, and 16:9, representing the ratio of the width of a horizontal image to its vertical height. This setting does not affect just the shape of the image; it also determines how many megapixels an image can contain. When the aspect ratio is set to 4:3, the maximum resolution of 10 MP is available; when the aspect ratio is set to 3:2, the greatest possible resolution is 9.5 MP; at 16:9, the greatest possible is 9. Also, the very lowest possible resolution, 0.3 MP, is possible only at the

121

4:3 aspect ratio. So if for some reason you need to take thousands of pictures and don't care if the quality is low, you may need to set the aspect ratio to 4:3 to achieve the lowest possible resolution and the highest possible number of recordable images. If you want your image to use the entire area of the LCD screen, choose 3:2, which is the aspect ratio of the screen. With 4:3, there will be black bars at the sides of the screen as you compose your shot; with 16:9, there will be black bars at the top and bottom of the screen.

Finally, one other option for aspect ratio was made available with the upgrade to firmware version 2.0, although you can't set it with the aspect ratio switch. Panasonic has provided a 1:1 aspect ratio, yielding a square image, which is accessible through the Recording menu, on a new line below Digital Zoom. Just navigate to that line and set the 1:1 Aspect item to On. Then, all images you take will be square. This option can be useful if you know ahead of time that the image will be used in a square format. Or, you might just prefer the square shape for aesthetic reasons. Of course, you can always achieve a 1:1 aspect ratio after the fact, using software such as Photoshop.

Autofocus Switch

The Autofocus switch is located on the left side of the lens barrel as you hold the camera in shooting position. Its three selections are Autofocus, Autofocus Macro, and Manual Focus. I previously discussed Autofocus and Manual Focus, but Autofocus Macro needs more discussion. When you move the switch to select this mode, focusing changes to a macro range. So, instead of the normal range of 1.64 feet (50 cm) to infinity at wide angle, the lens can focus as close as 0.4 inch (1 cm). It is a good idea to set the flash to Off when using macro mode, because the flash would not be useful at such a close range. I'll discuss macro shooting in more detail in Chapter 8.

Flash Switch

The flash switch is on top of the camera at the far left. It has only one function -- to unlatch the flash mechanism so it can pop up and be available in case conditions call for its use. If you, the user, do not manually pop the flash unit up using this switch, it will not be available, because the camera cannot pop the unit up automatically.

Mode Dial

The Mode dial is on top of the camera to the right of the hot shoe as you hold the camera in shooting position. We discussed this dial extensively in Chapter 3. Its settings move you between the various modes of shooting: Intelligent Auto, Program, Aperture Priority, Shutter Priority, Manual, Custom 1,

123

Custom 2, Motion Picture, and Scene. If you happen to leave the Mode dial in a position that does not select one of those settings, the camera will display a message advising you that the dial is not in a proper position.

Shutter Button

This control is quite familiar by now. You press it down halfway to check focus and exposure, and press it the rest of the way to record the image. You can also press it to wake the camera up from Power-Save mode. The shutter button has a somewhat different use when you are making multiple exposures using that option on the Recording menu. After the initial exposure is made, you move to the next one by pressing the shutter button halfway down.

Zoom Lever

The Zoom lever is a ring with a ridged handle that encircles the shutter button. The lever's basic function is to change the lens's focal length between wide-angle, by pushing it to the left, toward the W indicator, and telephoto, by pushing it to the right, toward the T indicator. The lever also has some other functions. When you are viewing pictures in Play mode, the lever enlarges the image on the LCD screen when pushed to the right, and selects different numbers of images to view when pushed to the left. In addition, when you are playing a motion picture taken by the camera, the Zoom lever can be used to raise and lower the audio volume. Also, you can use this lever to speed through the menus a full page at a time.

Focus Button

The Focus button is on the top of the camera to the right of the shutter button, at the far right of the camera as you hold it in shooting position. As we discussed earlier, this button is used to move the focusing frame around the screen, so you can focus on an object that is not in the center of the screen. To do this, you aim the camera, press the Focus button, then use the cursor keys to move the frame to wherever you want it. Then press the center button in the five button array (Menu/Set) to set the location. To return the frame to the center of the screen, press the Focus button again, then press the Display button on the lower left of the camera back's controls.

The Focus button has one other function that we mentioned briefly earlier. When you set the camera to Manual Focus, the standard focusing procedure is to use the joystick to adjust the focus until it looks the way you want it on the screen. However, even with the camera set to Manual Focus, if you press the Focus button the camera will attempt to focus automatically. If you are faced with a tricky focusing situation, such as a subject that has important points to focus on at various distances, using the Focus button to pre-focus the subject can give you a starting point, from which you can take over with the joystick to fine-tune the focus as you want it.

125

Power Switch

There isn't a lot to say about the power switch, but I didn't want to leave any controls out, and this is a good opportunity to discuss the Power-Save feature. The power switch is on the far right of the camera's top. You move it to the right for On and to the left for Off. When you do either of these actions, the little green status light blinks briefly to acknowledge the action.

If you leave the camera unattended for a period of time, it automatically powers off, if this option is set through the Setup menu. We'll discuss the Setup menu in Chapter 7, but this option can be set to be off altogether so the camera never turns off just to save power, or it can be set to turn the camera off after two, five, or ten minutes of inactivity. You can cancel the Power-Save shutdown by pressing the shutter button.

Record - Playback Switch

This switch is located directly to the right of the top of the LCD screen. In the up position, the switch puts the camera into Recording mode; in the down position, it puts the camera into Playback mode. I find that it can sometimes be a good idea to leave the switch in Playback mode to avoid the situation when you turn the camera on in recording mode without taking off the lens cap. When you do that, the camera balks and tells you to remove the lens cap and press the right cursor button before proceeding. If the camera is in Playback mode, you can turn it on with the lens cap on and it will be happy as a clam, because the lens does not extend outward and hit the lens cap.

Joystick

The little joystick on the back of the camera (just below the Record - Playback switch), has quite a few functions, of which we have discussed several. It is used to adjust the focus when the camera is in Manual Focus mode. It is used to adjust shutter speed and/or exposure when the camera is in Aperture Priority, Shutter Priority, or Manual Exposure mode. But it has many other duties as well, described below.

Exposure Compensation with Joystick

The joystick can be used as an alternative way to adjust exposure compensation. The standard way to dial in exposure compensation is to press the up button in the five-button array on the back of the camera, the button that is marked with the dark plus sign and white minus sign. Then you use the left and right cursor keys to set the amount of positive or negative exposure for the image.

To use the joystick for the exposure compensation adjustment, you start by moving the joystick to the left. At that point the joystick navigation icon, a circle with protruding arrows in the bottom right corner of the screen, will have its arrows turn red and point up and down, indicating that you can now adjust exposure compensation by moving the joystick up and down. You will also see the little icon for exposure compensation, with the plus and minus signs, in the lower left corner of

127

the screen. Moving the joystick up and down at this point will raise and lower the level of exposure compensation.

Program Shift with Joystick

Here is a function of the joystick that is not immediately obvious. I don't think you'd find this one without reading the manual (or this book), unless you are a very thorough experimenter. Program Shift is available only in Program mode. What this function does is let you take the camera's automatic settings for aperture and shutter speed and reset them to a different combination that yields the same exposure. That is, you can "shift" both settings the same amount in opposite directions. For example, if the camera computes the correct settings as f/2.0 at 1/100 second, you can shift those settings to any equivalent pair that would yield the same exposure, such as f/2.2 at 1/80 second, f/2.5 at 1/60 second, f/2.8 at 1/50 second, or f/3.2 at 1/40 second.

Why would you want to do this? You might want a slightly faster shutter speed to stop action better, or a wider aperture to blur the background more, or you might have some other creative reason. Of course, if you really are interested in setting a particular shutter speed or aperture, you probably are better off using Aperture Priority mode or Shutter Priority mode. However, having the Program Shift capability available is a good thing for a situation in which you're taking pictures quickly using Program mode, and you want a quick way to tweak the settings somewhat.

Here's how to use Program Shift. When you're about ready to take a picture, press the shutter button halfway to calculate the exposure. Then release the button, and you will see a yellow rectangle that outlines the values for shutter speed and aperture at the bottom of the LCD screen. Within a few seconds, press the joystick up or down to shift the values.

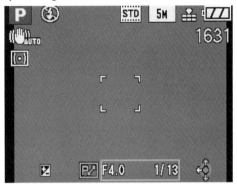

You will see the new values within the rectangle, and the Program Shift icon (a rectangle with a P and a diagonal two-headed arrow) will appear at the bottom of the screen to indicate that Program Shift is in effect. To cancel Program Shift, use the joystick to change the settings until the Program Shift icon disappears. Also, turning off the camera will cancel Program Shift.

Getting Access to Quick Menu with Joystick

The little joystick is not done yet; it offers another complete set of tricks if you take it in another direction by pressing in on it. This function—getting access to the Quick menu—is not entirely obvious from the user's manual, so let me emphasize that point. You put your thumb on the joystick's knob and push in, as if the joystick were a push-button, which, of course, it is. You have to press fairly hard, but once your press has registered, a mini-version of the camera's menu system opens up at the top of the screen. You navigate right and left with the joystick across the menus until you find the category you want, then move up and down that category with the joystick until you hit the exact selection you want, then you press in firmly on the joystick to select it.

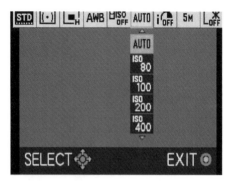

The options available through the Quick menu vary by the mode the camera is in. Not surprisingly, the Quick menu offers the most choices in Program, Aperture Priority, Shutter Priority, or Manual mode. It offers the smallest variety in Intelligent Auto mode: only AF Tracking on or off, Picture Size, and LCD power-saving options. There are a moderate number of choices in Scene mode and Motion Picture mode. (The Quick menu is not available at all in Playback mode.)

Is the Quick menu preferable to using the Recording menu system? It's a matter of personal choice. You may find the Quick menu to be useful for choosing certain options, such as ISO or White Balance. It's a good idea to experiment a bit.

AF/AE Lock Button

AF-AE
Lock
Button

The AF/AE Lock button is located just to the right of the

joystick on the camera's back. As I discussed in Chapter 4, through the Recording menu's settings you can select whether this button locks both autofocus (AF) and auto-exposure (AE), or only one or the other. You just press the button to lock whichever settings have been selected through the menu. Press it again to unlock. You cannot lock exposure with the button when the camera is set to the Manual Exposure recording mode.

Five-Button Array

What I call the five-button array is the set of five buttons on the back of the camera, just below the Joystick and the AF/AE Lock button, arranged in a pattern that looks a bit like the leaves of a clover, set on a circular platform. You could also call the outer buttons cursor buttons. The center button is often called the Menu/Set button. Its main functions are to make selections and to enter and exit from menus.

The cursor buttons act as cursor keys do on a computer keyboard, letting you navigate up and down and left and right through the various menu selections. The right key is also the one to press if you turn the camera on in Recording mode without removing the lens cap; the camera scolds you with a message telling you to remove the lens cap and press that key.

The top, or up, button, besides its cursor duties, is also used to play the audio that has been recorded along with a still image, and to play a motion picture that was recorded by the camera.

The buttons' functions do not stop there. Each of the cursor buttons performs at least one additional function, as indicated by the icon on the button. Let's go through those functions, starting at the top and moving clockwise.

Top Button: Exposure Compensation, Auto Bracket, Multi Aspect, Flash Output

The top button is a real workhorse, tackling no less than four separate photographic (as opposed to navigation or menu-selection) functions: exposure compensation, Auto Bracket, Multi Aspect, and Flash Output. We'll discuss each of these adjustments in turn.

Exposure Compensation

We discussed this function in some detail in Chapter 2. When you are in Recording mode, press the top button once and the camera displays a scale showing Exposure Value (EV) increments, negative and positive. Use the right and left buttons to maneuver along this scale, and press the center button to choose a value to vary the exposure. Remember that you have to reset this value once you no longer need it, because the camera will retain this adjustment indefinitely otherwise.

Auto Bracket

Press the top button twice, and you are presented with the Auto Bracket screen. Auto Bracket is a function that lets you take three exposures with one press of the shutter button, at three different exposures, thereby giving you an added chance of getting a good, usable image. If you're shooting with RAW Quality, exposure is not so much of an issue, because you can adjust it later with your software, but it's always a good idea to get the exposure as correct as possible.

Once you enter the Auto Bracket screen, you adjust the size of the EV interval between exposures with the right and left cursor buttons. You spread the interval further apart with the right button, and narrow it with the left button. The maximum spread between exposures is 3 EV levels. The first picture taken is always at the metered level, or 0 change in EV; the second is at the lower EV (darker), and the third is at the higher EV (brighter).

The Auto Bracket procedure cannot be used with flash (either built-in or external); the flash will be forced off and cannot be activated. Auto Bracket is not available with Intelligent Auto mode or Motion Picture mode, nor with several of the Scene mode categories. Auto Bracket cannot be set in Manual or Shutter Priority mode if the shutter speed is set to be longer than one second. Auto Bracket is canceled when the camera is turned off.

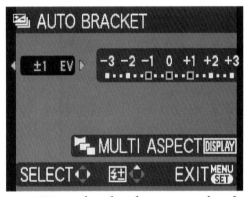

One more note: Remember that the camera takes three exposures in quick succession, but they are not simultaneous, so you need to be sure to hold the camera steady until all three images are recorded, if you're not using a tripod.

Finally, note that the LX3 also provides white balance bracketing, which was discussed earlier in connection with other white balance settings. That type of bracketing is controlled through the white balance setting screen, and not through the exposure bracketing screen.

Multi Aspect

Multi Aspect is similar to Auto Bracket, in that it lets you take multiple images with one press of the shutter button, but this time the result is images with different aspect ratios. You don't have to select anything other than the function itself, because the camera automatically records images using all four available aspect ratios: 4:3, 3:2, 16:9, and 1:1. However, it only includes the 1:1 aspect ratio if the 1:1 Aspect option has been turned on in the Recording menu.

To activate the Multi Aspect function, press the top button twice to reach the Auto Bracket screen, then press the Display button (the lowest button on the back of the camera, just to the right of the screen), which toggles between Auto Bracket and Multi Aspect modes. This brings you to the Multi Aspect screen. Press the right or left button to change the setting for Multi Aspect from Off to On, or vice-versa, then press the Menu/Set button to exit.

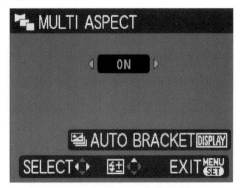

Now you will see a screen with three or four (if 1:1 is turned on) different colored rectangles outlining the frames for the three (or four) aspect ratios. When you press the shutter button, you will take the same image in all of those aspect ratios.

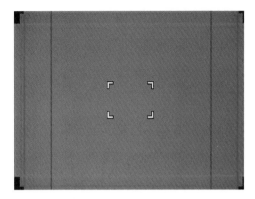

One thing that can be a bit confusing about Multi Aspect is that you will hear only one shutter activation, so it will sound as if only one picture is being taken, but the camera actually records all three (or four) images with the single shutter sound.

Multi Aspect cannot be used at the same time as Auto Bracket, and Multi Aspect is not available when you are shooting with RAW quality. (This can be confusing, because the camera will let you set both Multi Aspect and RAW, but only one image will be recorded when you press the shutter button.) Multi Aspect, like Auto Bracket, is canceled when the camera is turned off.

Flash Output

This is a nice capability to have. Flash Output lets you lower or raise the intensity of the flash, which can be useful in situations in which the subject is very small, or reflectivity is high.

Flash Output is controlled by the top button, the same one that activates Exposure Compensation, Auto Bracket, and Multi Aspect. Press the top button three times, and you are presented with the flash intensity screen.

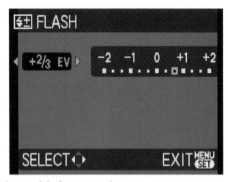

Use the right and left cursor buttons to increase or decrease the EV of the flash up to 2 full levels in either direction. This setting, unlike Auto Bracket and Multi Aspect, stays in place even when the camera is turned off and then back on. So you need to be careful to reset the flash output adjustment to zero (unchanged) when you are done with it. The LCD screen will help you remember that it's set on, though, by displaying an icon showing the amount of positive or negative flash output value, in the upper left of the screen, just to the right of the image stabilization icon. The Flash Output adjustment is not available when using the Flash Burst setting in Scene mode.

One aspect of this function is that the Flash Output control works fine with external flash units that are attached to the LX3's hot shoe, if they operate automatically in TTL (through-the-lens light metering) mode and communicate properly with the camera. With such external flash units, you can raise or lower the output of the flash in exactly the same way as with the built-in flash unit. I have tested this operation with Panasonic's own flash for the LX3, the DMW-FL220, and the Metz Mecablitz 48 AF-1 flash unit for Olympus and Panasonic cameras. Flash functions such as this will also work with other compatible flash units, such as the Olympus FL-36R.

Right Button: Flash

The right button does double duty as the Flash control. The button will not operate any flash functions unless the built-in flash unit is popped up or the hot shoe has a flash unit inserted in it that communicates with the camera and is turned on. Also, as we discussed in Chapter 2, the button will not work if the camera is set to Intelligent Auto mode.

If the built-in flash unit is popped up in a mode such as Program, then, if you press the Flash button, you are presented with a list of several options on the screen that you can scroll through by repeatedly pressing the Flash button, by using the up and down cursor buttons, or by pressing the joystick up and down.

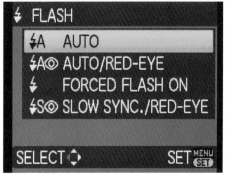

The four options (in Program mode) are Auto Flash, Auto Flash with Red-Eye Reduction, Forced Flash On, and Slow Sync with Red-Eye Reduction. Note that the list does not include Forced Flash Off, because you can choose that option by stowing the flash unit back inside the camera. Also note that this list has all four options only in Program and Aperture Priority modes; in other modes, fewer options are available.

There's one other option that ordinarily does not appear on the menu: Forced Flash On with Red-eye Reduction. That option only appears in two contexts: when you are in Scene mode, with the scene type of Party or Candle Light. Otherwise, that option is not available for you to choose.

If you place into the hot shoe on top of the camera a flash unit that speaks the LX3's language and turn it on, then pressing the Flash button gives you as many as five options, including Forced Flash Off.

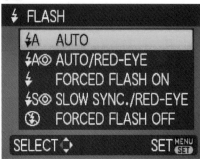

You could turn off the external flash unit using its own power switch, but for some reason the camera is programmed to let you force the external flash off through the camera's menu system, even though you can't turn off the built-in flash unit in this way. You have to push the built-in flash unit back down into the camera to force it off.

In Chapter 8, I'll talk about when to use the various flash modes.

Down Button: Fn

The "down" button in our clockwise group bears the label "Fn." To me, this is the "function" button, though some people prefer to call it the Fn button without drawing conclusions about its meaning. In any event, here is how it works.

The default (factory) setting for the Fn button is to give you a way to quickly review a shot without switching from Recording mode into Playback mode. For example, if you have just snapped a picture and you want to check it out on the LCD display while still in Recording mode, press the Fn button and the last recorded image will appear on the screen. In this mode, called Review in the user's manual, you can zoom the displayed picture up to eight times its normal size with the Zoom lever, scroll through other pictures with the left and right cursor buttons, and delete pictures using the Trash button. The image stays on the screen for about ten seconds; then the camera reverts to Recording mode. Because the camera is still in Recording mode, you cannot get access to the more advanced operations available on the Playback menu, such as Dual Play, Slide Show, and Category Play. You also can't play any audio memo that was recorded with the image, and you can't play motion pictures using the Review function.

If you don't care about having the Review function available, you can set the Fn key to give you access to any one of several other menu operations from the Recording menu: Film Mode, Sensitivity, White Balance, Metering Mode, AF Mode, Intelligent Exposure, or 1:1 Aspect. Just go into the Setup Menu, navigate to Fn Button Set, and then make your choice from the list that appears. Note that the camera has to be set to Recording mode when you do this, or the option for Fn Button Set will be grayed out. The camera presumably does this because the only options available to set the Fn Button to carry out are functions from the Recording menu. You cannot set the Fn button's action while the camera is in Intelligent Auto mode or Scene mode.

Left Button: Self-Timer

The last button on our clockwise tour of the cursor buttons, the leftmost button, operates the camera's self-timer. The self-timer is very easy to use on the LX3. Just press this button, then select a time from the menu that appears. For many modes, the selections will be Off, 10 seconds, or 2 seconds. Select the one you want with the up and down buttons. The LCD screen will then have an icon on it showing the self-timer with the chosen number of seconds beside it.

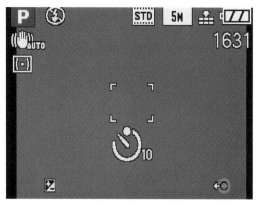

Now you can wait as long as you want before actually taking the picture (unless the camera times out with Power Save or you take certain other actions, such as changing the Recording mode). Compose the picture, then press the shutter button. The AF Assist lamp, which does double duty as the self-timer lamp, will blink and the camera will beep, until the picture is recorded at the end of the specified time. The beeps and blinks speed up for the last second as a warning, when the time is set to ten seconds. For the two-second operation, the camera just beeps and blinks four times rapidly. You can cancel the shot while the self-timer is running by pressing the center button (Menu/Set).

It's not a bad idea to set the camera to take a burst of pictures, so you'll have several choices after the self-timer has done its work. You need to use the Burst button (discussed below) to do that, though, because the self-timer does not work with the Hi-speed Burst setting of Scene mode. It also doesn't work in Motion Picture mode, and you cannot set it to 2 seconds in Intelligent Auto mode or to 10 seconds in the Self Portrait setting of Scene mode.

Display Button

The Display button is a round button at the bottom left of the camera's back, below the five-button array. It has several functions, depending on the context. If you have the LX3 set for still recording, in any mode other than Intelligent Auto, here is the progression you get from repeated presses of the Display button: (1) full display, showing information including battery life, ISO, recording mode, and number of pictures that can be shot with the remaining storage, as well as the histogram (discussed later), if that option is turned on through the Setup menu; (2) blank display except for the focus area; and (3) focus area, grid lines for composition, and histogram, if that option is on.

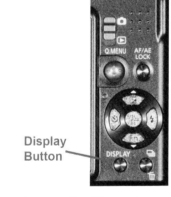

Display
Button

If the camera is set to Intelligent Auto mode, the display button produces the screens listed above, but the histogram does not appear, even if it is turned on in the Setup menu.

If the camera is set for Playback, repeated presses of the Display button produce the following screens: (1) the recorded image with time and date, image number, and basic information including film type; (2) the same information, with the

141

addition of the shutter speed, aperture, and recording mode, as well as the histogram if that option is turned on through the Setup menu; and (3) just the recorded image, with no other information.

If you are playing back a motion picture, the display is similar, except for some added information that applies to that mode, including a brief display showing that the Zoom lever controls the audio volume.

The Display button also has several other functions: You can press it to move the focus area back to the center of the screen if you have moved it off center either by having pressed the Focus button or by having used the Recording menu system for moving the focus. Also, this button is used to select pictures you are marking for deletion after pressing the Trash button (see discussion just below) and selecting Delete Multi. During a slide show, the Display button toggles the display of image numbers and slide show controls on and off. In Title Edit mode (discussed in Chapter 6), the button toggles between displays of various types of characters, and it toggles between the Auto Bracket and Multi Aspect modes. The button also displays information about the settings that have been saved to the C2 Custom Memory Set storage areas, and it displays information about each of the Scene types when you are viewing them in the Scene menu.

Burst/Trash Button

This button is in the far right corner on the bottom of the camera's back. It is labeled with two icons: an overlapping stack of rectangles, representing a burst of shots, and a trash can.

Burst Function

When the camera is set to Record, this button triggers Burst mode, in which the camera presents you with three further options for rapid shooting: Off, Normal, and Unlimited. Off means no burst of shots is selected. Normal means the camera will take a small number of shots; and Unlimited means that, under certain conditions, the camera will keep taking still pictures indefinitely until the storage card is filled up, as long as you hold down the shutter button.

There are a few points you need to bear in mind about using this button for this purpose. The main thing to realize is that you are not going to get a super burst of shots just by pushing this button and selecting one of the options. Several variables will affect how much of a burst you will actually get, including the Quality setting, the Picture Size setting, and whether the flash is operating.

Here are some guidelines. Shooting RAW images in Program mode with no flash and the burst mode set to Normal, you may get three shots in your burst. If you set the burst to Unlimited, you will still get only three shots when shooting RAW. In Normal mode, the rate of shooting will be about 2.5 frames per second.

If you want to have a really long burst of shots, you need to set the Quality to Fine or Standard and leave the flash undeployed. Then, when you hold the shutter button down, you will get a continuous burst at about 2 frames per second initially. After a while you will notice that the frame rate slows down somewhat; the timing for this change depends on resolution, quality, and the type of storage card being used. But the burst will continue for as long as you have space on the card. Some photographers have used this function for a limited sort of time-lapse photography, importing a very long series of still images into video editing software and playing it back at the normal video speed of 24 or 30 frames per second, for example, to show a construction project seemingly completed at super speed.

If you want to take a burst of shots with flash, there are two ways to accomplish this. However, you cannot do this by setting Burst mode with the Burst button and using the camera's built-in flash. If you try to do this, and then push the flash button to turn the flash on, the camera will force the flash off and display the flash-off icon. If you then try to turn the flash on using the Flash button, the camera will display an error message. However, if you have a compatible external flash that communicates with the camera through the hot shoe, you can use Burst mode with that flash. You can get three pictures in your flash burst (and no more), shooting RAW or any other quality.

Another way to set the camera for continuous shooting is to rely on the settings in Scene mode for Hi-speed Burst and Flash Burst. The latter setting is the only way to get any burst of shots with the built-in flash operating. Also, using Scene mode ensures that the optimum settings are used to achieve the greatest possible burst. The assumption is that if you choose this mode, you have made a decision that quantity and speed of shooting are considerably more important than the quality of the shots, and the camera's burst settings in Scene mode will make the necessary adjustments to achieve quantity and speed.

There are some other limitations to Burst mode. First, the focus is locked in when the first picture is taken. Exposure and White Balance are locked in by the first picture when the camera is set to Normal burst, but they will vary with each shot in the Unlimited mode. When the self-timer is set, the burst is limited to three shots, even in Unlimited mode. Also, you have to remember to cancel Burst shooting yourself, because the camera will leave it set on until you turn it off, even after the camera has been turned off and on again.

Trash Function

When the camera is set to Playback mode or you have activated the Review function using the Fn button in Recording mode, the Burst/Trash button takes on the identity of the trash can. Press the button and you are presented with several options on the LCD screen: Delete Single Yes/No, Delete Multi, and Delete All. Use the cursor buttons to navigate to your choice. If you select Delete Single Yes, then the camera will delete the image that is currently displayed on the screen.

If you select Delete Multi, then the camera presents you with a display of recent pictures, up to six at a time per screen. You then move through them with the cursor buttons, and press the Display button to mark any picture you want to be included in the group for deletion. You can press Display a second time to unmark a picture for deletion. When you are finished marking pictures for deletion, press Menu/Set to start the deletion process; the camera will ask you to confirm, and one more press of Menu/Set will carry out the deletion of all of the marked images. Delete All, of course, deletes all images, unless you have marked some as Favorites and choose to delete all except Favorites (indicated by stars). You can interrupt a deletion process with the Menu/Set button, though some images may already have been deleted before you press the Menu/Set button.

Chapter 6

Advanced Topics — Playback

If you're like me, you take the images you've created and import them into your computer, where you manipulate them with software, then post them on the web, print them out, e-mail them, or do whatever else the occasion calls for. In other words, I don't spend a lot of time viewing the pictures in the camera. But that doesn't mean it's not a good thing to know about. Depending on your needs, there may be plenty of times when you take a picture and then need to examine it closely in the camera. Also, the camera can serve as a viewing device like an iPod or other gadget that is designed, at least in part, for storing and viewing photos. So it's worth taking a good look at the advanced playback functions of the LX3.

Let's start with a brief rundown of the basic playback techniques. To quickly review a recently taken still picture, press the Fn button (the bottom button in the five-button array), assuming you have not changed its default setting of Review.

For more robust playback of images, with more options available, move the Record-Playback switch (to the right of the top of the LCD screen), to its down position for Playback. Then scroll through the images with the left and right cursor buttons in the five-button array.

That's Playback reduced to the very basics, and that's really enough to let you view your images and show them to others with no problems. But there are considerably more options to choose from, so let's explore the nuts and bolts.

The Playback Menus

Yes, if you spotted the "s" at the end of "Menus" in the above heading, you are observant. But no, that was not a mistake. There is only one Recording menu, but there are two Playback menus. This situation could lead to some confusion, so let's sort through it carefully.

As you know, when the camera is in Recording mode and you press the Menu/Set button, you enter the menu system. Once in that system, you can navigate to either the Recording menu or the Setup menu, or, if you have selected Scene recording mode from the Mode dial, you can also enter the Scene menu to select a particular type of scene.

But if the camera is in Playback mode when you press Menu/ Set, you encounter a slightly different proposition. Here you can navigate to the Playback Mode menu, the Playback menu, or the Setup menu.

The first option, the Playback Mode menu, allows you to se-lect from these options: Normal Play, Dual Play, Slide Show, Category Play, and Favorite Play. (Favorite Play shows up only when the Favorites features has been activated through the Playback menu.) This Playback Mode menu option is similar to the Mode dial on top of the camera, which selects among the various Recording modes. There was no room for a Play-back Mode dial, and its existence probably would have been confusing, so the Playback Mode selection is done through this separate branch of the menu system.

The second option on the menu system is the actual Playback menu, which lets you set various options for how playback works. (A third menu option available when in Playback mode is the Setup menu, which is discussed in Chapter 7.)

Now let's look at the two different Playback-related menus, one at a time.

The Playback Mode Menu

The first option once you enter the menu system when the camera is in Playback mode offers five choices: Normal Play, Dual Play, Slide Show, Category Play, and Favorite Play.

Normal Play

Normal playback is fairly straightforward. With this mode selected, you scroll through the images individually using the left and right cursor buttons. Whenever an image is displayed on the screen, you can press the Trash button to initiate the deletion process, and choose to delete either a single image, multiple ones, or all images. If you want to mark some images as Favorites, which will be useful for the Favorite Play mode and can single out some images to be saved from deletion, you first have to make sure the Favorite function is activated by selecting Favorite in the Playback menu (*not* the Playback *Mode* menu) and setting that option to On. Then, when you are dis-

148

playing an image in Normal Playback mode, press the down button (Fn button) to mark it as a Favorite. A star will then be displayed on the screen for that image.

Dual Play

The second option for Playback mode is Dual Play. When you select this mode of playback, the camera places two images together on the screen and places a yellow frame with up and down arrows on one of them, along with a left or right arrow.

The display is rotated, so both pictures can fit on the screen in their normal shapes, and the cursor butons take on new functions with respect to their directions as a result.Use the up and down (normally left and right) arrows to select the picture to go in that frame, and move the frame to the other image with the left or right arrow, and then use the up and down arrows to select the image for that frame. Once you have the two images you want on the screen together, you can compare them, using the Zoom lever on top of the camera to enlarge them as needed for the comparison process. You can delete either of the images by pushing the Trash button, then following the prompt asking if you really want to delete it.

Slide Show

The third option on the Playback Mode menu is Slide Show. Navigate to this option, then press Menu/Set, and you are presented with the choices All, Category Selection, and Favorite.

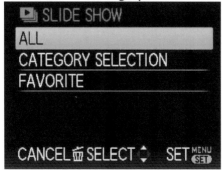

The last two choices are dependent on whether you have pictures that are marked as Favorites or that fall into Categories, as discussed later.

Play All

If you choose All, you are taken to a menu with the choices Start, Effect, and Setup.

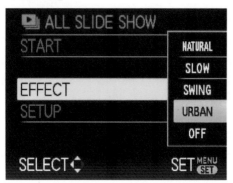

You can choose Start to begin the slide shovw, or you can go to Setup or Effect first and make some selections. Setup lets you choose a duration of 1, 2, 3, or 5 seconds for each image, but you can only set the duration if Effect is set to Off. That is, if you select any effect, the camera will automatically set the duration to 2 seconds per image. You can also choose to set music On or Off, and repeat On or Off.

For effects, you have the following choice of styles: Natural, Slow, Swing, Urban, or turning effects off altogether. If you choose Urban, the camera not only plays "urban" music, it uses a somewhat more dramatic visual style, with a variety of transitions, including converting some color images to black and white. So choose Urban only if you're a free-spirited type who doesn't mind a slide show with altered slides.

Once the slide show has begun, you can control it using the five-button array as a set of playback controls, the same as with playing back motion pictures. The up button controls play/pause; the left and right buttons move back or forward one slide when the show has been paused; and the down button is like a stop button; pressing it ends the slide show. A small display showing these controls stays on the screen during the show, along with image numbers, unless you press the Display button to switch to a screen showing the images only.

Category Selection

Besides playing all of the pictures available, you can select the images by category. You don't get to place your pictures in categories of your own making; the camera has a pre-defined list of nine groups that it considers "categories," and it plays all of the images in whichever single category you select. Note that some of the categories overlap with others; that is, an image might be in more than one category. Here are the categories:

• All images from the following Scene types: Portrait, Soft

Skin, Self Portrait, Night Portrait, and Baby 1 and 2

- All images from the following Scene types: Scenery, Sunset, Aerial Photo

- All images from the following Scene types: Night Portrait, Night Scenery, Starry Sky

- All images from the following Scene types: Sports, Party, Candle Light, Fireworks, Beach, Snow, Aerial Photo

- All images from the following Scene types: Baby 1 and 2

- All images from the following Scene type: Pet

- All images from the following Scene type: Food

- All images with a Travel Date

- All motion pictures

Favorite

The third and final option for selecting the images to play in a slide show is to play all of the images that you have marked as Favorites. In order to use this option, you have to have first turned the Favorite setting on in the Playback menu. Then, when you play the images normally, you press the down button to mark an image as a Favorite. Press the same button to remove the Favorite setting from an image.

Other Playback Modes

This next part could be confusing, so I'll try to explain carefully. We have just finished talking about one of the Playback Mode options called Slide Show, which includes within its own options the choices of playing the slides by Category or by Favorites. We are now moving on to discuss Playback Mode options other than Slide Show. Those other modes happen to include playing all images by Categories or by Favorites. The difference is that, in these modes, unlike Slide Show mode, the images do not advance by themselves, and there are no music options or transitions playing along with them.

Category Play

In Category Play, you select any one of the nine categories listed earlier. You are now viewing this subset of your images. You can move through them with the left and right cursor buttons, and you can delete them using the normal delete procedure, using the Trash button. You can change the amount of information displayed using the Display button.

Favorite Play

In this Playback mode, the camera will play back pictures marked as Favorites. As noted earlier, you have to turn on the Favorite function in the Playback menu, and you have to have marked at least one picture as a Favorite.

Playback Menu

Okay. We have discussed Playback Mode generally, and we have discussed the Playback Mode menu, which lets you select among the various Playback modes: Normal Play, Dual Play, Slide Show, Category Play, and Favorite Play.

Now we are going to talk about the *other* Playback menu. We just finished talking about the Playback Mode menu; this next one is just the Playback Menu. If you recall, this one is similar to the Recording Menu, because it offers a collection of options for how Playback works. To enter this menu system, first set the camera to Playback mode with the Record-Playback switch. Then press the Menu/Set button, which takes you into the menu system. Make sure the cursor is in the far left column of the menu display, then press the down button to highlight the green triangle, which signifies the Playback menu. Then press the right button to enter the list of menu options, and scroll down to the one you want.

I will talk about each one in order, from top to bottom. Note that not all options are available in a given Playback mode. They are all available for Normal playback, but some are not available for Category Play or Favorite Play. (You can't enter the Playback menu system at all while in Dual Play or Slide Show Play.)

Calendar

The first Playback menu option for Normal play is Calendar. Highlight that line of the Playback menu, then press the right button to activate the Calendar display. This option presents you with a calendar showing the current month (assuming, of course, that you have set the date accurately). Any date on which an image was recorded has a small image showing. Scroll through the dates with the left and right buttons. You can select any of those dates using the Menu/Set button. When you do, the camera displays the pictures from that date. You

154

then can scroll through them and display any of them on the full screen.

Title Edit

This is the second operation available through the Playback menu. It allows you to enter normal text, numerals, punctuation, and a fairly wide range of symbols and accented characters for a given image or group of images through a system of selecting characters from several rows. I won't go into all the details of using this system, because it's easy enough to figure out by working through it yourself. One point to be aware of is that you can toggle between three displays of capital letters, lower case letters, and numerals and symbols using the Display key. The maximum length for your caption or other information is thirty characters.

Once you have entered the title or caption for a particular image, it does not show up unless you use the Text Stamp function, discussed below. The title is then attached to the image, and it will print out along with the image. There is no way to delete the title other than going back into the Title Edit function and using the Delete key from the table of characters, then deleting each character until the title disappears.

Text Stamp

The Text Stamp function takes information associated with a given image and attaches it to the image in a visible form. For example, if you have entered a title or caption using the Title Edit function discussed above, it does not become visible until you use this Text Stamp function to "stamp" it onto the image. Once you have done this, the text or other characters in the title will print out if you send the picture to a printer. Besides the information entered with the Title Edit function, the Text

Stamp function gives you the choice of making the following other information visible: year, month, and day; year, month, day, and time; age of subject (if set); travel date (if set). Also, you can apply this function to information from pictures taken with Scene types Baby 1 or 2 and Pet, if you have entered a name for your baby or pet.

Resize

This function from the Playback menu can be useful if you don't have access to software that can resize an image, and you need to generate a smaller file that you can attach to an e-mail message or upload to a web site. You activate the Resize function using the standard procedure with the cursor buttons, then select whether to resize a single image or multiple ones. Next, use the cursor buttons to select what size to reduce the image to, down as far as 0.3 MP, depending on the aspect ratio of the image. One important point to note is that this function does not overwrite the existing image; it saves a copy of it at a smaller size, so the original will still be available. The new images will be found at the end of the current set of recorded pictures. Another point: RAW images, protected images, and motion pictures cannot be resized, nor can still pictures with audio recordings attached, or pictures stamped with Text Stamp.

Trimming

This function is similar to Resize, except that, instead of just resizing the image, the camera lets you crop it to show just a portion of the original image. To do this, you select Trimming from the Playback menu, use the Zoom lever to enlarge the image, and use the cursor buttons to view the part of the image you want to retain. Then press the Menu/Set button to lock in the cropping, and reply to the camera's prompt by selecting Yes

156

when it asks if you want to save the new picture(s). Again, as with Resize, the new image will be saved at the end of the current set of recorded images, and it will have a smaller size than the original image, because it will be cropped to include less information (fewer pixels) than the original image. The Trimming function cannot be used with RAW images, protected images, motion pictures, still pictures with audio recordings attached, or pictures stamped with Text Stamp.

Leveling

This is an interesting function; it allows you to make minor corrections in the rotation of an image. For instance, if you have a straight object in your image that is slightly off-kilter, you can apply a small amount of clockwise or counter-clockwise rotation to correct the tilt. When you select this function, the camera displays a framework of horizontal and vertical grid lines to help you make fine adjustments.

You then carry out the rotation with the left and right cursor buttons. As with all of the modifications made through the Playback menu, there are several limitations. First, the correction is limited to two degrees positive or negative rotation. Second, the process achieves the rotation effect in part by zooming in and cropping the image slightly, so a part of the image is lost and the size of the file and the resolution will decrease somewhat. Finally, as with the Resize and Trimming functions, this operation cannot be carried out with RAW images, protected images, motion pictures, still pictures with audio recordings attached, or pictures stamped with Text Stamp.

Aspect Conversion

Here is another modification you can apply to recorded images in the camera. This one lets you take a still image taken in 16:9 aspect ratio and convert its aspect ratio to 3:2, 4:3, or 1:1. When you select the function, the camera presents you with a yellow rectangle that you move around with the cursor buttons to select the part of the widescreen image that you want to keep in the modified image with the new aspect ratio. This operation can be done only on images taken in the 16:9 aspect ratio. As with the other modifying operations discussed above, this operation does not work with RAW images, protected images, motion pictures, still pictures with audio recordings attached, or pictures stamped with Text Stamp.

Rotate

This option on the Playback menu lets you rotate images in increments of 90 degrees, either clockwise or counter-clockwise. When you have an image displayed, enter the Playback menu, select Rotate, then select either the right-facing or left-facing Rotate arrow that appears on the screen. You can perform this action repeatedly until you have rotated the image to the desired orientation. This function, unlike those discussed above, does work with RAW files and still images recorded with audio, but it does not work with motion pictures or protected pictures. Also, this function, unlike the others discussed above, does not save a new image; it actually just rotates the existing image. Of course, you can always rotate it again to restore it to its normal orientation, so the function is non-destructive.

Rotate Display

This option, like the Rotate option, does not modify the image. It can be set to either Off or On, and affects the way the camera displays images for which you held the camera in a vertical position when you recorded the image—that is, images for which the top of the camera was rotated to be facing to the right or left when you took the picture. If you leave this option turned off, then those images will be displayed to look the way they were viewed when they were taken; that is, you will have to rotate the camera back to a vertical position to see such images properly. If you turn this option on, then the camera automatically displays those images in a vertical orientation when the camera is held horizontally. To do this it has to shrink the image so the entire vertical image will fit within the horizontal screen.

The Rotate Display function does not work when you are viewing multiple images on the screen; or when you have pressed the zoom lever to the left (toward the W setting) to view images 12 or 30 at a time, or by date from the calendar.

Favorite

We have mentioned this function a couple of times before, because you have the option of viewing just your Favorite pictures under some of the Playback modes. Here is how to select an image as a Favorite. You select the Favorite option from the Playback menu, and turn it on. Then, when you are viewing pictures on the LCD screen, you can press the down button to mark the image as a Favorite. If you are viewing with the information display turned on, you will see a star, the symbol for Favorite, in the lower right corner of the screen with a down-pointing triangle next to it, indicating that pressing the down button will select (or de-select) the displayed image as

159

a Favorite.

When you select an image as a Favorite, a star appears in the upper left corner of the image. If you de-select the image as a Favorite, the star disappears. You cannot select RAW quality images as Favorites.

DPOF Print

The next option on the Playback menu, DPOF print, standing for Digital Print Order Format, is a process that was developed by the digital photography industry to allow users of digital cameras to specify, on the camera's own memory card, which pictures to print and other details, then take the card to a commercial printing shop to have them printed according to those specifications.

With the LX3, you select this option from the Playback menu, and then select Single or Multi. If you select Multi, the camera gives you a display of six images at a time on the screen. Using the four cursor buttons, you navigate through the images. When you arrive at one you want to have printed, you press the Menu/Set button, and you then see a box with the word "Count" followed by a number and up and down arrows. You use the up and down cursor buttons to raise (or, later, lower, if you change your mind) the number of copies of that image you want to have printed. In addition, if you press the Display button, the word "Date" is added to the small image for that picture, and the date will be printed on that picture. You can follow the above procedure for a single image by selecting "Single" when you first enter the DPOF option.

If you want to use the DPOF system to print photos recorded on the camera's built-in memory, you need to copy them to a memory card and then take that card to the printing store, after setting the DPOF options. (See the Copy function, discussed later in connection with the Playback menu.)

The DPOF settings cannot be set for RAW images.

Protect

The next Playback menu option is Protect, which is used to lock selected images against deletion. The process is essentially the same as that for the Favorite function; you enter the Playback menu system, select the Protect option, then select Multi or Single. You then mark the images you want to protect, using the Menu/Set key. When a picture is protected in this way, a key icon appears on the left side of the image.

The Protect function works for all types of images, including RAW files and images with audio recordings. Note, however, that all images, including protected ones, will be deleted if the memory card (or camera's built-in memory) is re-formatted.

Audio Dub

This procedure on the Playback menu gives you the capability of recording a brief audio snippet for an image that was previously recorded. After you select Audio Dub from the Playback menu, you press the right cursor button, which takes you to a screen showing an icon of a microphone, and advising you to press Menu/Set to start. Press Menu/Set, and the microphone icon flashes while ten little triangles proceed from left to right, indicating the ten-second time for recording. After ten seconds, the recording ends, unless you press Menu/Set to end it sooner. Then you can move to other images to record audio, or you can cancel out of this process with the Trash button, followed by pressing Menu/Set to exit the menu system.

161

The Audio Dub function does not work with RAW images, motion pictures, or protected files. There is no way to adjust the volume of these audio recordings while they are playing, but you can adjust the speaker volume generally through the Setup menu, using the Volume option to raise and lower the volume for all purposes.

Copy

The final option on the Playback menu is the Copy function, which you can use to copy images from the camera's built-in memory to an SD storage card, and vice-versa. After you select Copy from the Playback menu, press the right cursor button to pop up the little sub-menu, which provides two options, represented by two pairs of icons connected by a directional arrow. One icon has the label "In," showing that it represents the camera's built-in memory; the other has the label "SD," representing an SD card inserted into the camera. One pair of icons has an arrow going from the In icon to the SD icon, and the other pair has the arrow going from the SD icon to the In icon.

If you select the first icon, the camera will prompt you with a message asking you to confirm whether you want to copy the images from the built-in memory to the memory card. If you choose Yes to confirm, the process starts, if there are images to copy.

If you select the second pair of icons, the camera displays an image, and asks if you wish to copy it to the camera's built-in memory. If you select Yes, the camera copies that single image to the built-in memory. You can then move on to other images, or cancel out of the process with the Trash button.

Remember that the built-in memory has a capacity of only

about 50 MB, so it does not hold very many high-quality images.

Connecting to a Television Set

The LX3 is quite capable when it comes to playing back its still images and videos on an external television set. The camera comes with an audio-video cable as standard equipment. The cable has a mini-USB connector at one end and two composite, or RCA, connectors at the other end. The white RCA plug is for audio (the camera's sound is monophonic, not stereophonic); the yellow one is for composite video.

To connect the cable to the camera, you need to open the little door on the right edge of the camera (when held in shooting position). Be careful to plug the small (mini-USB) connector into the middle one of the three ports inside the door; there is one other port that the connector would fit into, but that one is for external power, not audio and video.

AV Out/USB Port

You then need to connect the yellow and white connectors to the composite video and audio inputs of a television set. You may then need to set the TV's input selector to Video 1, or AUX, or some other setting so it will switch to the input from the camera.

Once the connections are set and the TV is turned on with the

163

PHOTOGRAPHER'S GUIDE TO THE PANASONIC LUMIX LX-3

correct input selected, turn on the camera in Playback mode, and you can play back any images or video you have recorded. HD video will play back with no problems on a standard television set (though not in HD quality, of course). You may need to switch the camera's aspect ratio to achieve the proper result on screen.

You can also purchase the optional component video cable to connect the camera to a high-definition television set. In that case, you will have five plugs to connect to the TV: one each for the red, blue, and green components of the video, and two for the left and right channels of the audio. However, the audio is still monophonic, even though it is output in two channels. At this writing, the component cable costs between $90.00 and $100.00, so unless you have a clear need for high-definition images on the TV screen, you may want to settle for the very adequate quality offered by the standard-equipment composite video cable.

Once you have connected the camera to a TV set, the camera operates very much the same way it does on its own. Of course, depending on the size and quality of the TV set, you will likely get a much larger image, possibly better quality (on an HD set), and certainly better sound. This difference will be especially noticeable in the case of slide shows; the music sounds much better through TV speakers than from the camera's minuscule speaker.

One side note: When the camera is connected to a TV with the standard video cable, it can not only play back recorded images; it can also record. When it is hooked up to a TV while in recording mode, you can see on the TV screen the live image being seen by the camera. So you can use the camera as a video camera of sorts, and you can use the TV screen as a large monitor to help you compose your photographs.

Chapter 7
The Setup Menu

N ow we have discussed the options available to you in the Recording and Playback menu systems (including options in the Scene branch of the menu system). The third and final menu system is the Setup Menu. As a reminder, you enter the menu systems by pressing the Menu/Set button (the center button in the five-button array on the lower half of the camera's back). The available menus change depending on whether you're in Recording mode, Playback mode, or Scene mode. However, no matter what other options are available, you can always enter into the Setup menu. After you first press the Menu/Set button, press the left cursor button to get into the left column of menu choices, then use the down button as many times as needed (one or two) to get down to the wrench icon, indicating the Setup menu. Once the wrench is highlighted, press the right button to get back into the list of menu choices, which will now contain the Setup choices. Let's look at those choices in turn.

Clock Set

With the Clock Set option highlighted, press the right button to take you to the settings screen. Just follow the arrows. If you see an item that needs to be adjusted, use the up and down arrows to adjust it. Then move to the next item with the right button. When the settings are all correct, press Menu/Set to exit and save. You can always cancel with the Trash button.

165

World Time

This is a handy function when you're traveling to another time zone. Highlight World Time, press the right button to access the next screen, and use the up button to highlight Destination. Then use the left and right buttons to scroll through the world map and select the time zone you will be traveling to. The map will show you the time difference from your home time. Press Menu/Set to select this zone for the camera's internal clock. Then, any images taken will reflect the correct time in the new time zone. Go back into the World Time item and select Home to cancel the changed time zone setting.

Travel Date

This function lets you set a range of dates on which you will be taking a trip. The purpose of this capability is to record on which day of the trip each image was taken. So when you get back from a vacation trip, if you use the Text Stamp function to "stamp" the recorded data on the images, the images will show they were taken on Day 1, Day 2, etc., of the trip. The entries are self-explanatory; just follow the arrows and the camera's prompts.

Beep

This menu option lets you adjust several sound items. First is the volume of the beeps the camera makes when you press a button, such as when navigating through the menu system. You can set the beeps to Off, Normal, or Loud. It's nice to be able to turn the beeps off if you're going to be in an environment where such noises are not welcome.

Second is the tone of the beeps. Check out the three possibilities and see which one you like best.

Third is the volume of the shutter operation. Again, it's good to be able to mute the shutter sound.

Finally, you can choose from three shutter sounds.

Volume

With this option, you adjust the volume of the camera's speaker for playing back motion pictures and images recorded with audio files. This setting does not affect the sound level for beeps and shutter operations, which is controlled separately, as noted above.

Custom Set Memory

This is a useful function for anyone who wants to have a quick way to set several shooting parameters without having to remember them or go into menus and fiddle with switches to set them. The camera lets you record four different groups of settings, each of which can be recalled immediately by setting the Mode dial to C1 or C2. You can consider this function a way to create four of your own custom-tailored Scene types for use whenever you want them.

Here is how this works. First, you need to have the camera set to Recording mode, so slide the Record-Playback switch to its upward position, for Recording. Then, set the Mode dial on top of the camera to the shooting mode you want to select: Program, Aperture Priority, Shutter Priority, or Manual. (You can't use Intelligent Auto mode in a Custom setting.) Next, make any other adjustments that you want to have stored for quick recall such as Film Mode, ISO, autofocus method, exposure metering method, white balance, and the like. You can set most of the items on the Recording Menu and the Setup Menu for inclusion in the custom settings.

Once you have all of the settings as you want them, leave them that way and enter the Setup menu. Navigate to Custom Set Memory and press the right button, which gives you choices of C1, C2-1, C2-2, and C2-3. For your most important group of settings, choose C1, because that group of settings is the easiest to recall quickly. Once you have highlighted the memory slot number you want to use to save your current settings to, press Menu/Select, and the camera will ask you to confirm that you want to overwrite any existing settings that were saved to that slot.

When you go to use your saved settings, just turn the Mode dial to C1 or C2. If you choose C1, you're done; the camera is now set as it was when you selected the C1 slot to save your settings to. If you choose any of the other three groups of settings (C2-1, C2-2, or C2-3), you will also need to select the second part of the number (1, 2, or 3) from a short menu. Once you have selected the custom mode you want, you are still free to change the camera's settings, but those changes will not be saved into the Custom Set Memory unless you enter the Setup menu again and save the changes there with the Custom Set Memory option.

If you want to see what settings you have saved for any of the three C2 Custom Memory slots, the camera will display them for you. Turn the Mode dial to C2 and the camera will show you the menu for selecting one of the sub-settings for C2; either C2-1, C2-2, or C2-3. At the bottom of that screen you will see a small letter i, for "information," next to the label for the Display button. If you push the Display button, you will get information consisting of two screens that show the settings that the camera currently has saved for whichever of the three Custom settings is highlighted on the menu. Move between the two screens with the left and right buttons. (There is no such information display for the C1 settings.)

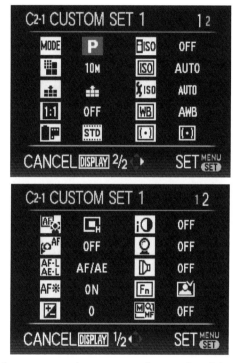

These are the 20 items that are saved in each of the three C2 slots:

Shooting mode

Picture Size

Quality

1:1 Aspect Ratio

Film Type

Intelligent ISO

Sensitivity

ISO Limit Set

White Balance

Metering Mode

Autofocus Mode

Pre Autofocus

AF/AE Lock

Autofocus Assist Lamp

Exposure Compensation

Intelligent Exposure

Digital Zoom

Conversion

Fn Button Set

Manual Focus Assist

There are a few limitations with this system. You cannot set certain parameters from the Setup Menu, but they are ones you would have no reason to include in a set of custom shooting parameters, such as Clock Set, Travel Date, and Reset. You cannot set certain items that require physically moving a switch, such as aspect ratio (other than 1:1, which is set from the menu) and manual focus. You should note that the camera saves only the items listed above; you can't save settings like a specific shutter speed or aperture. But apart from those limitations, Custom Set Memory is a powerful capability, and anyone who has or develops a favorite group of settings would be well advised to experiment with it and take advantage of its power.

Fn Button Set

We discussed this option earlier, in connection with how to play back images. This button, which is the down, or bottom button of the five-button array on the back of the camera, is initially set to Review, which means you can press this button while in Recording mode to play back recent still pictures. You can also set this button to carry out any one of several other functions from the Recording menu instead. The available functions besides Review are Film Mode, Sensitivity (ISO), White Balance, Metering Mode, AF Mode, Intelligent Exposure, and 1:1 Aspect Ratio. For example, if you often have a need to change your ISO setting, you might want to assign that operation to the Fn button for ease of access.

Monitor

This item on the Setup menu lets you adjust the brightness of the LCD display in seven steps. This brightness setting takes effect even if you use the LCD Mode setting, discussed below.

LCD Mode

This setting also involves the brightness of the LCD display. It has three settings: Off, Auto Power LCD, and Power LCD. The Off setting does not turn off the LCD display; instead, it means that the Power LCD setting is off, and the LCD display is at its normal brightness. The Auto Power LCD setting means that the screen's brightness will adjust according to the ambient lighting conditions. Finally, in the Power LCD mode, the screen becomes extra-bright to compensate for brightness that makes it hard to see the screen. This mode dims back to normal after 30 seconds; you can press any button to make the screen turn bright again. An indicator appears at the left of the LCD display, toward the bottom, if Power LCD or Auto Power LCD mode is active. That indicator is an asterisk (*) for Power LCD and an asterisk with an A (A*) for Auto Power LCD.

You should note that using either Power LCD or Auto Power LCD mode decreases the battery's endurance because of the use of extra power to make the screen brighter. If you find it hard to see the screen in bright sunlight and don't want to use an external viewfinder, you might want to try the Power LCD approach to see if the added brightness gives you enough visibility to compose your shots properly.

Guide Line

This option gives you some control over the grid lines that are displayed on the LCD screen to assist you with composition of your pictures when you cycle through the various screens with the Display button. Once you select Guide Line from the Setup menu, you get to a screen with three options: Recording Information, Pattern, and Position. If you set Recording Information on, when the grid lines are displayed, along with the grid lines there will be information about the shooting mode, ISO setting, and other data. Otherwise, you will see only the grid lines, unless you have the histogram turned on, in which case you will see the grid lines and the histogram (see below).

The pattern of the grid lines is controlled by your selection on the Pattern option. There are two patterns to choose from: a grid that forms nine equal rectangles on the screen, or a pattern with sixteen equal rectangles as well as two diagonal lines that intersect at the exact center of the screen. The second pattern is useful to find the center point of the image. When the camera is in Intelligent Auto mode, the grid lines cannot be changed from the standard nine-block pattern.

Finally, if you select Position, you have the option of adding a different set of two grid lines to the LCD display in Recording mode. To do this, select Position and set it to On. You then will have a set of two intersecting lines displayed on the LCD when you select this screen using the Display button. In other words, a new screen is added to the cycle of displays, as follows: full recording information; no recording information; guide lines with the selected pattern; and guidelines whose position can be adjusted with the cursor buttons. When the screen with the two lines is displayed, use all four buttons to position the lines as you want, then press Menu/Set to lock them in that position.

Histogram

This option controls whether or not the histogram displays on the screen. The menu option has only two choices: On or Off. If you turn the histogram on, it will display on the right side of the LCD screen in both Recording mode and Playback mode for every image (if the Display button has been used to display the screen that includes the histogram). The histogram does not display in Intelligent Auto or Motion Picture mode.

What is a histogram? It's a graph, or chart, representing the distribution of dark and bright areas in the image that is being displayed on the screen. The darkest blacks are represented by vertical bars on the left, and the brightest whites by vertical bars on the right, with continuous gradations in between. On the LX3, when the Histogram option is turned on, the histogram shows up as a small box on the right side of the screen, with a jagged array of white vertical lines that reach to various heights and that spread across the screen in differing patterns, depending on the brightness of the image.

If you have a histogram like the one below, in which the pattern of white lines in the box resembles a tall ski slope coming from the left of the screen down to ground level in the middle of the screen, that means that there is an excessive amount of black and dark areas in the image (tall bars on the left side of the histogram), and very few bright and white areas (no tall bars on the right).

A ski slope like the one below, moving from the middle of the screen up to the top of the right side of the screen means just the opposite — too many bright and white areas.

174

A histogram that is "just right" would be one that starts low on the left, gradually rises to a medium peak in the middle of the screen, then moves gradually back down to ground level at the right. That pattern indicates a good balance of whites, blacks, and medium tones. An example of this pattern is shown below.

The histogram is an approximation, and should not be relied on too heavily. It may be useful to give you some feedback as to how evenly exposed your image is likely to be. (Or, for playback, how well exposed it was.)

175

Highlight

When you turn this feature on, the camera produces a flashing area of black and white on areas of the image that are over-saturated with white, so they may be too bright. The flashing effect takes place only when you are viewing the pictures in Auto Review, Review, or Playback mode. That is, when the image appears briefly on the screen after it has been recorded (Auto Review), when you use the Review function by pressing the Fn button, assuming you have the Fn button set to the Review function in the Setup menu, or when you play the pictures in normal Playback mode. The purpose of this feature is to alert you that your picture may be washed out (overexposed) in some areas, so that you may want to reduce the exposure for the next shot.

Lens Resume

This setting has two sub-options: zoom resume and manual focus resume, either of which can be turned on or off. If you turn on zoom resume, then, after you turn the camera off and back on, the lens will return to its last zoom position. If you leave this setting turned off, the lens will zoom out to its widest angle when the power is turned back on.

If you turn manual focus resume on, then the camera will return to its previous manual focus position after the power has been turned off and back on, or after the camera has been switched off of manual focus and back, or has been switched to Playback mode and then back to Recording mode. If you leave this setting turned off, the manual focus will go to the infinity setting when the power is turned back on or one of the other conditions occurs.

Manual Focus Assist

We discussed this feature briefly earlier, in talking about how to use Manual Focus. This function lets you decide whether and how the screen display is magnified when you're using Manual Focus. With the MF Assist option highlighted, press the right cursor button to pop up the little sub-menu that lets you choose among the three available options: Off, MF1, and MF2. If you choose Off, there is no magnification; MF1 is the setting for magnification of the center of the screen; MF2 is the setting for magnification of the whole screen.

You may want to experiment with Manual Focus using each of these three options, then settle on the one that works best for you, and leave that setting in place. I tend to prefer MF2, which magnifies the whole screen and seems a bit easier to use, but one of the others may work better for you.

Economy

This menu option gives you two ways to save battery power: Power-Save and Auto LCD Off. Power-Save turns the camera off after a specified period of not using any of the camera's controls. The period can be set to two, five, or ten minutes, or the option can be turned off, in which case the camera never turns off automatically (unless it runs out of power).

Auto LCD Off, which can be set to fifteen or thirty seconds, turns off the LCD screen after the specified time. This option can also be turned off altogether, so the screen never goes dark. If the screen is blanked through this feature, the small green status light, just below the joystick, turns on to let you know the camera is still on and operating, even though the screen is dark. You can press any button to turn the screen back on.

Auto Review

This option gives you control over how your pictures are reviewed immediately after they have been recorded by the camera. The possible settings are Off, 1 second, 2 seconds, Hold, and Zoom. These are fairly self-explanatory; after the shutter button is pressed, the image appears on the screen (or not) according to how this option is set. If you set it to Hold, the image stays on the screen until you press any button; if you set it to Zoom, the image is displayed for one second, then enlarged four times and displayed on the screen for one additional second.

One note: the user's manual says that Hold keeps the picture on the screen until you press "any button." That may be true, but if you press some buttons, such as the Self-timer or Burst buttons, you will be activating a new operation, so you're better off relying on the Menu/Set button for this purpose.

Note that Auto Review is automatically activated, regardless of the setting through the Setup menu, in certain shooting modes: Auto Bracket, Multi Aspect, Multi Film, Hi-Speed Burst, and Flash Burst.

Auto Review does not work with Motion Picture mode.

Number Reset

This function lets you reset the folder and image number for the next image to be recorded in the camera. Use this option if you want to choose the folder and image numbers for your pictures, rather than letting the camera assign them. You can assign a folder number between 100 and 999 and the number of the first image in the folder will be set to 1.

Reset

This function resets all Recording mode settings to their original states, and also resets all Setup menu settings to their original states.

USB Mode

If you are going to connect the camera directly to a computer or printer, you need to go into this menu item and select the appropriate setting: PC (for connecting to a computer), Pict-Bridge (for connecting to a printer that allows direct printing), or Select on Connection. If you choose Select on Connection, you don't select the setting until after you have plugged the USB cable into the device to which you are connecting the camera. The LX3 connects to a computer using the rapid USB 2.0 connection standard, assuming your computer has a USB port of that speed. (If not, the camera will still connect at the slower speed of the computer's older USB port.)

Video Out

This menu option is not available on the LX3 version that is manufactured for the United States market. In other areas, this option lets you choose whether the video signal sent to a TV set is compatible with the NTSC or PAL standard. NTSC is used in the United States, Japan, and some other areas; PAL is used in Europe and many other locations.

TV Aspect

This menu option applies only when you are connecting the camera to a television by means of the audio-visual cable. The only two choices are 16:9, for widescreen, or 4:3, for fullscreen.

m/ft

This option gives you the choice of meters or feet for the units of distance used by the camera on the display, such as when you are using Manual Focus.

Scene Menu

This option has two possible settings: Off or Auto. If you choose Auto, whenever you turn the Mode dial on top of the camera to the SCN setting to select Scene mode, the LCD display will immediately display the menu of Scene modes with one of them highlighted, so you can scroll through them and choose. For example, it may start with Portrait highlighted, so you can press the Menu/Set button to select Portrait, or you can scroll through the other choices to find the one you want. This method saves you the step of entering the menu system and selecting the Scene menu.

If, instead, you turn the Scene Menu setting off, when you turn the Mode dial and select Scene mode, the screen displays the image the camera sees in whatever Scene type happens to be the last one used; if you want to select a different Scene type, you need to press Menu/Set and navigate to the Scene menu to make a different selection.

I like the Auto setting, because chances are I will want a different Scene type than the one I used when I last turned the Mode dial to SCN. But if you often choose the same Scene type, you may prefer to leave this setting off, and go back to the same Scene type each time you select SCN on the Mode dial. It's not hard to enter the menu system and choose a different Scene type, if you need to.

Menu Resume

This menu item can be set either on or off. When it is turned on, whenever you enter the menu system, the camera displays the last menu item you had selected. When it is turned off, the camera always starts back at the top of the first screen of the menu system, which may be the Recording menu, Playback menu, or Scene menu, depending on what mode the camera is in (Recording, Playback, or Scene mode).

User's Name Recording

This menu item lets you enter your name (or any other name), so that, if this option is turned on, that name will be recorded along with the image, giving you a record of who took the picture. The name cannot be seen on the images in the camera; you have to use Panasonic's supplied PHOTOfunSTUDIO-viewer software to make sure the name was recorded correctly.

Version Display

This menu item has no settings; when you select it, it displays the version of the camera's firmware that is currently installed. As I write this, my camera has version 2.2 of the firmware installed. (That is the version that ships with the camera at this time; the latest version available for download is 2.1.)

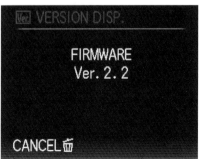

Firmware is a term for something that is somewhat like both software and hardware; it is the electronic programming for the camera's circuitry, and is electronically recorded into the camera, either at the factory, or through your computer if you upgrade the firmware with an update provided by Panasonic. A new version of the firmware can fix bugs and can even provide new features, so it's well worthwhile checking the Panasonic web site periodically for updates. Instructions for installing an update are provided on the web site. Essentially, the process involves downloading a file to your computer, saving that file to an SD card formatted for the camera, then placing that card in the camera so the firmware can be installed.

Format

This is one of the more important menu options. Choose this process only when you want or need to completely wipe all of the data from a memory storage card. When you select the Format option, the camera will ask you if you want to delete all of the data on the card. If you reply by selecting Yes, it will proceed to do so, and the result will be a card that is empty of images, and is properly formatted to store new images from the camera.

If you want to format the camera's built-in memory, you have to remove any card from the camera, so the built-in memory is the only possible memory to be formatted.

Language

This option gives you the choice of language for the display of commands and information on the LCD screen. The choices are English, German, French, Spanish, Italian, and Japanese. If the camera should be set to a language you cannot read, just go the Setup menu and select the next-to-last option on the menu, then press the right button and scroll up or down until you find the language you want.

Demo Mode

This last option on the Setup menu lets the camera perform two demos. The first is a demonstration of the camera's optical stabilization system, giving a graphic demonstration of how much that system can counteract the effects of camera shake.

The other demo is a self-running demo that shows off some of the camera's features, with some sample images. Note: This is one of the few areas in which the LX3 differs from its sister camera, the Leica D-Lux 4. The D-Lux 4 does not have this auto demo available.

Chapter 8
OTHER TOPICS
Macro (Closeup) Shooting

Macro photography is the art or science of taking photographs when the subject is shown at actual size (1:1 ratio between size of subject and size of image) or slightly magnified (greater than 1:1 ratio). So if you photograph a flower using macro techniques, the image of the flower will be about the same size as the actual flower. You can get wonderful detail in your images using macro photography, and you may discover things about the subject that you had not noticed before taking the photograph.

This branch of photography is not just for flowers, insects, and other wonders of nature. It can also be very useful for mundane matters such as copying a receipt or memo you need to take with you to another office; for copying materials in a library (while observing applicable copyright laws, of course), or for taking pictures of your furniture to the carpet or paint store to find matching colors. You will undoubtedly find other uses, once you realize what a superb capability this camera has for making sharp closeup images of just about anything.

To use the LX3's macro mode, you have only one basic setting to change: Move the autofocus switch on the left side of the lens barrel to its middle position, for Macro Autofocus, with the tulip icon, indicating macro.

With the autofocus switch in Macro position, the camera is able to focus as close as 0.4 inch (1 cm) from the subject, when the Zoom lever is pushed all the way to the wide-angle setting. With the lens zoomed in to the full extent of optical zoom, the camera can focus as close as about 1 ft (30 cm) in Macro mode. If the camera is not set to Macro mode, then the closest focusing point is about 1.64 ft (50 cm) at the widest angle, and about 3.28 ft (1 meter) with the lens zoomed in fully.

You don't have to use the Macro setting to take macro shots; if you set the camera to Manual Focus by moving the focus switch to its lowest position (MF), you can also focus on objects very close to the lens. You do, however, lose the benefit of automatic focus, and it can be tricky finding the correct focus manually. Also, if you have the camera set to Intelligent Auto mode and move very close to your subject, the camera should detect the macro situation and automatically switch into Macro mode.

When using the Macro setting, you should use a tripod, because the depth of field is very narrow and you need to keep the camera steady to take a usable photograph. It's also a good idea to take advantage of the self-timer or a cable release (See Appendix B). If you take the picture using the self-timer or cable release, you will not be touching the camera when the shutter is activated, so the chance of camera shake is minimized. You should also leave the built-in flash retracted, so it can't fire. Flash from the built-in unit at such a close range would be of no use. If you need the extra lighting of a flash unit, you should consider using a special unit designed for close-up photography, such as a ring flash that is designed to provide even lighting surrounding the lens.

Although there is no ring flash made specifically to work with the LX3, there are flash units that could be used or adapted for this purpose, such as the Metz 15 MS-1 Ringlight. There are also other creative solutions to the problem of providing even lighting for closeup photography. For an excellent discussion of this and related issues, see *Closeup Shooting* by Cyrill Harnischmacher (English translation published by Rocky Nook 2007).

One question you may have is: If the camera can focus down to one centimeter and out to infinity in Macro mode, why not just leave it set in Macro mode? The answer is that in Macro mode, the focusing system is set to favor short distances, and it is not as responsive in focusing on farther objects. Therefore, in Macro mode you will notice that it is more difficult to focus on subjects at farther distances. The conclusion is that you should set the camera to Macro mode only when taking extreme closeups.

Using RAW Quality

We've already discussed RAW a couple of times. RAW is a

Quality setting in the LX3's Recording menu. It applies only to still images, not to motion pictures. When you set the Quality to RAW, the camera records the image without any in-camera processing; essentially, it just takes in the "raw" data and records it.

There are both pros and cons to using RAW in this camera. First, the cons. A RAW file takes up a lot of space on your memory card, and, if you copy it to your computer, a lot of space on your hard drive. Second, there are various functions of the LX3 that won't work when you're using RAW. The user's manual does not list all of these, but as far as I could determine, these are the functions that don't work with the RAW setting: Intelligent Exposure, Intelligent Auto mode, Digital Zoom, Audio Recording, Audio Dub, Multi Aspect, White Balance Bracket, High Dynamic Scene Mode, Multi Film, Resize, Trimming, Leveling, Aspect Conversion, Favorite, and DPOF (printing directly to a photo printer). Third, you may have problems working with RAW files on your computer, although those can be overcome.

Let's talk about the benefits provided by using RAW in this camera, and how much (or little) to worry about the drawbacks. The main benefit is that RAW files give you an amazing amount of control and flexibility with your images. When you open up a RAW file in a compatible photo-editing program such as Adobe Photoshop, or Photoshop Elements, the software gives you the opportunity to correct problems with exposure, white balance, color tints, and other settings. For example, on the next page is an example of how the information from a RAW file from the LX3 looks when initially opened in Adobe Photoshop CS5 on a Macintosh computer.

If you had the aperture of the camera too narrow when you took the picture, and it looks badly underexposed, you can manipulate the Exposure slider in the software and recover the image to a proper exposure level. Similarly, you can adjust the white balance after the fact, and correct color tints. You can even change the amount of fill lighting. In effect, you get a second chance at making the correct settings, rather than being stuck with an unusable image because of unfortunate settings when you pressed the shutter button.

The drawbacks of using RAW are either not too severe, or they are counter-balanced by the great flexibility RAW gives you. The large size of the files may be an inconvenience, but the increasing size of hard drives and SD cards, with steadily dropping prices, makes file size much less of a concern than previously. Some photographers don't like the difficulties of having to process RAW files on the computer. I have had problems with RAW files not loading when I didn't have the latest Camera RAW plug-in for Adobe Photoshop or Photoshop Elements, but with a little effort, you can download an updated plug-in and the software will then process and display your RAW images. The LX3 comes with SILKYPIX Developer Stu-

188

dio, a program for processing RAW files, so you don't have to buy any additional software to process those files.

The bottom line is you certainly don't have to use RAW, but you may be missing some opportunities if you avoid it. For further exploration of this topic, an exellent resource is *Camera Raw 101*, by Jon Canfield.

Using Flash

As we discussed in Chapter 5, the Flash button (aka the right cursor button) controls the various settings: Auto, Auto/Red-eye Reduction, Forced On, Slow Sync/Red-eye, Forced On/ Red-eye Reduction (available only with the Party and Candle Light varieties of Scene mode), and Forced Off.

We can break down the choices as follows: First, decide if you want to allow the flash to fire at all. If you don't want to, then don't pop up the built-in unit and don't attach an external unit. (Remember, there are some cases in which you can't make that decision because the camera won't let you. The obvious one is the Flash Burst setting in Scene mode. If you choose that setting without popping up the flash or attaching an external flash, the camera will not let you press the shutter button.)

If you decide to allow the use of flash, you may have some further decisions to make, depending on what shooting mode you're using. If you're using Intelligent Auto mode, once you've popped up the flash (or attached an external one), your flash decision-making is done. In that recording mode, the Flash button won't even operate; the camera automatically selects Auto mode for the flash, will determine whether to fire it, and, if so, whether to use Slow Sync and/or Red-eye reduction.

If you're using some of the scene types, the camera will also make the flash decisions for you. For example, in Fireworks and Starry Night modes, the flash is forced off, even if it's popped up. In the Portrait modes it's initially set to Auto with Red-eye Reduction, though you can use the Flash button to change the setting to Auto or Forced On.

To take back some of the decision-making authority from the camera, let's assume you're shooting in Program mode. Now you have to decide whether to choose Auto, Auto with Red-eye Reduction, Forced On, or Slow Sync with Red-eye Reduction.

Let's start with Forced On. Why would you want to force the flash to fire, when you could set it to Auto and let the camera decide whether it's needed? One case is when there is enough backlighting that the camera's exposure controls could be fooled into thinking the flash isn't needed. If, in your judgment, the subject will be too dark for that reason, you may want to force the flash to fire. Another such situation could be an outdoor portrait for which you need fill-in flash to highlight your subject's face adequately.

What about Slow Sync with Red-eye Reduction? Slow Sync means that the camera sets a relatively slow shutter speed, so that the ambient (natural) lighting will have time to register on the image. In other words, if you're in a fairly dark environment and fire the flash normally, it will likely light up the subject (say a person), but because the exposure time is short, the surrounding scene may show up as black in your image. If you use the Slow Sync setting, the slower shutter speed allows the surrounding scene to be visible also.

The other aspect of this setting is Red-eye Reduction. Red-eye is a familiar problem in color photos of people taken with flash. If the subjects are sitting in a dark place, their pupils are likely dilated, and the sudden bright flash bounces off of the red blood vessels in their retinas, giving an unnatural red tint to their eyes. When Red-eye Reduction is set, the camera fires a quick pre-flash before the picture is taken. The idea is that that flash will cause the subjects' pupils to contract, reducing the chance of the red-eye effect.

The other two choices in Program mode are Auto and Auto with Red-eye Reduction. Auto gives the camera a chance to use its programming to determine the best setting. It may set Red-eye Reduction and/or Slow Sync, depending on conditions. If you choose Auto with Red-eye Reduction, the flash will fire only if needed, but if it does, it will fire twice to reduce red-eye.

There are a great many considerations that go into the use of flash. The best advice I can give you is to consult an expert if you want to explore the subject further. An excellent book about the use of flash is *Mastering Digital Flash Photography*, by Chris George (Lark Books, 2008).

Infrared Photography

In a nutshell, infrared photography lets the camera record images that are illuminated by infrared light, which is invisible to the human eye because it occupies a place on the spectrum of light waves that is beyond our ability to see. In some circumstances, cameras, unlike our eyes, can record images using this type of light. The resulting photographs can be quite spectacular, producing scenes in which green foliage appears white and blue skies appear eerily dark.

Shooting infrared pictures in the times before digital photography involved selecting a particular infrared film and the appropriate filter to place on the lens. With the rise of digital imaging, you need to find a camera that is capable of "seeing" infrared light. Many cameras nowadays include internal filters that block infrared light. However, some cameras do not, or block it only to a relatively small extent. (You can do a quick test of any digital camera by aiming it at the light-emitting end of an infrared remote control and taking a photograph while pressing a button on the remote; if the remote's light shows up as bright white, the camera can "see" infrared light at least to some extent.)

The LX3 is quite capable of taking infrared photographs. In order to unleash this capability, you need to take a few steps. The most important is to get a filter that blocks most visible light, but lets infrared light reach the camera's light sensor. (If you don't, the infrared light will be overwhelmed by the visible light, and you'll get an ordinary picture based on visible light.)

As with most experiments, there are multiple ways to accomplish this. For example, if you search on the internet, you will find discussions of how to improvise an infrared filter out of unexposed but developed (*i.e.*, black) photographic film.

A more certain, if more expensive way to make infrared photographs with the LX3 is to purchase an infrared filter, along with an adaptor that lets you attach the filter securely to the camera. There are adaptors available from Panasonic and other companies. I bought one from a company called Lensmates, which makes several accessories for the LX3. All such adaptors require you to unscrew the trim ring from the camera's lens, and screw on the adaptor in its place. You can then attach any filter or accessory lens with a 46mm diameter that screws on. (See Appendix B for more information about this and other accessories for the LX3.)

The filter I have seen most often recommended is the Hoya R72, and it is what I use. It is a very dark red, and blocks most visible light, letting in mainly infrared light rays in the part of the spectrum that tends to yield interesting photographs.

The next question is to figure out the exposure. Photographers have different approaches, and time spent looking on the internet for discussions of those approaches will be rewarding. I set a custom white balance, using brightly sunlit green foliage as the base. That is, I used the camera's White Balance menu setting in the Record menu, and, in the screen for setting a custom white balance, I aimed the camera at the bright green foliage and pressed the Menu/Set button. The results were essentially what I expected from infrared photography—scenes with tree leaves and grass that look white, and other unusual, but pleasing effects. One problem that may arise is the presence of a fairly large "hot spot" shaped like a hexagon, in the middle of your image. That happened with the image below, and I had to crop out half of the image to preserve what is shown here. If you see these spots in your images, you may be able to fix the problem by zooming in; I found fewer hot spots at longer focal lengths. If that doesn't work, you may have to compose the image so you can crop out the part with the offending spot.

For exposure, I set the camera to shoot in Aperture Priority mode and let it select the necessary long shutter speed. (The long shutter speed is necessary because of the dark filter.) I set the camera on a tripod and disabled the image stabilizer, because it is not needed when the camera is stabilized by a tripod. The LX3 did the rest. You can often get interesting results if you include a good amount of green grass and trees in the image, as well as blue sky and clouds.

Street Photography

One of the reasons many users prize the LX3 is because it is very well suited for street photography — that is, for shooting candid pictures in public settings, often surreptitiously. The camera has several features that make it a strong candidate for this type of work – it is lightweight and unobtrusive in appearance, so it can easily be held casually or hidden in the photographer's hand. Its 24mm equivalent wide-angle lens is excellent for taking in a broad field of view, for times when you shoot from the hip without framing the image carefully on the screen.

What are the best settings for street shooting with the LX3? Well, if you ask that question on one of the active Panasonic (or Leica) forums, you are, naturally, likely to get many different responses. I'm going to give you some fairly broad guidelines as a starting point. The answer depends in part on your own personal style of shooting, such as whether you will talk to your subjects and get their permission before shooting in a measured way, or will fire away from across the street with a palmed camera and hope you are getting a usable image.

At any rate, here is one set of guidelines that you can start with and modify as you see fit. To get the gritty "street" look, set Film Mode to Dynamic BW, but dial in -2 Noise Reduction and -1 Sharpening. Set Quality to RAW plus Fine JPG to give you post-processing options. Set aspect ratio to 16:9 to give a wide field of view. Set ISO to 400 to give you good image quality while boosting sensitivity enough to stop action with a fast shutter speed.

When you're ready to start shooting, go into Manual Focus mode and set the focus to approximately the distance you expect to shoot at, such as 6 feet (2 meters) on the MF scale. Then, when you're ready to snap a picture, use the Focus button on top of the camera to make a quick fine-tuning of the focus. Some street photographers maintain that this method is faster and more efficient than relying on the autofocus system. For exposure, set the camera to Aperture Priority mode, with the aperture set to about f/4.5. When shooting at night, you may want to open the aperture a bit wider, and possibly boost the ISO to 800. Of course, for any of this sort of shooting, you leave the lens zoomed back to the full wide-angle position. Finally, my own preference is to set the camera to burst mode, so it will take a series of shots when you hold down the shutter button; that gives me a better chance of getting a usable image, especially when I'm shooting from the hip.

Digiscoping

Digiscoping is the specialized practice of attaching a digital camera to a spotting scope in order to get clear shots of remote objects, generally birds and other wildlife. I haven't personally tried this with the LX3, though I did do some digiscoping with an older, heavier camera, with mixed results. I used a very good quality scope, a Swarovski Optik ATS 80 HD Scope with a 20-60x eyepiece, which was attached to the camera with a special adapter made to fit that scope. The main problem I encountered was fairly severe shakiness of the image, because, at the great magnification by that scope, the slightest bit of camera shake is very noticeable. With a fairly heavy camera, I found it to be difficult to get good images.

It's likely that you would get much better results using the LX3 with a good scope. The LX3 is a very lightweight camera, so it won't overbalance the scope. Also, it has an excellent lens and relatively large sensor, so the image quality should be excellent. Another significant point in favor of using the LX3 for this endeavor is that Leica, maker of the D-Lux 4 alter ego of the LX3, also makes spotting scopes. In fact, Leica even makes a digiscoping adapter designed to attach the D-Lux 4 to a Leica scope, so you can have a great degree of integration among the various pieces of equipment in your setup. See the links in Appendix C for some good sources of information about the equipment and techniques involved in this activity.

APPENDIX A
QUICK REFERENCE: HOW TOs

In this section, I'm going to set out a list of common tasks you might want to accomplish with your LX3, along with a series of steps you can take to get each task done as simply as possible. We'll be covering a good deal of familiar ground here, because we've already discussed how to carry out all of the basic camera operations. The difference here is that a list may come in handy if you're new to the camera, or haven't used it in a while and have forgotten how to operate some of the controls.

This is not a comprehensive list of photographic situations you may encounter; I have tried to list some typical ones that a new camera owner might run across. If you don't see what you need in this list, you might find an answer in the main text of this book.

One other note: Some of these steps assume that you have the camera's basic settings set a standard way. For example, that you have the Scene Menu setting in the Setup Menu set to Off. If some steps don't seem to work properly, there may be other Setup or other menu items that need to be adjusted.

Taking Pictures

First Steps

For all of the following tasks, the first thirteen steps are:

1. Remove lens cap

2. Move On-off switch to the On position

3. Move Record-play switch to the Record position

4. Check Aspect Ratio switch on top of lens barrel; make sure it is set how you want it (3:2 for picture shape like that of 35mm film; 4:3 for shape like standard TV screen; 16:9 for widescreen shape); check setting of 1:1 Aspect Ratio in Recording menu

5. Set Focus switch on left of lens barrel to top position, AF, unless otherwise noted

6. While in Record mode, press Menu/Set button to get access to Recording menu

7. Use up and down buttons to highlight Quality, if available; if not, go to step 11

8. Press right button to get access to sub-menu

9. Use up and down buttons to highlight top value; arrow pointing at six bricks

10. Press Menu/Set button to select that Quality (Fine)

11. Use up and down buttons to highlight Picture Size

12. Press right button to pop up sub-menu

13. Select largest value available (10M, 9.5M, or 9M); if grayed out, leave as is

General Picture-Taking in a Hurry

14. Turn Mode dial on top of camera to the Intelligent Auto setting (letters iA in camera icon)

15. Press Open button on top left of camera to pop up the built-in flash unit

16. Aim at subject, compose picture

17. Press shutter button on top right of camera

Indoor or Outdoor Portrait

14. Turn Mode dial on top of camera to the SCN setting

15. Press Menu/Set button to get access to Scene Mode menu

16. Press right button to highlight Portrait type of scene

17. Press Menu/Set to select Portrait type of scene

18. Press Open button on top left of camera to pop up the built-in flash unit

19. Aim at subject, compose picture

20. Press shutter button on top right of camera

Outdoor Scenery or Group Photo

14. Turn Mode dial on top of camera to the SCN setting

15. Press Menu/Set button to get access to Scene Mode menu

16. Press right button to highlight Scenery type of scene

17. Press Menu/Set to select Portrait type of scene

18. Aim at subject, compose picture

19. Press shutter button on top right of camera

Rapid-Fire Burst of Shots - No Flash

14. Turn Mode dial on top of camera to the Intelligent Auto setting (letter A in camera icon)

15. Press the Burst/Trash button (lowest button on right side of camera's back)

16. Press Down button twice to highlight Unlimited

17. Press Menu/Set button to select Unlimited

18. Aim at subject, compose picture generally

19. Hold down shutter button on top right of camera until finished with burst sequence

Rapid-Fire Burst of Shots with Flash

14. Use the Open button on top left of camera to pop up the built-in flash unit

15. Turn the Mode dial on top of the camera to the SCN setting

16. Press the Menu/Set button to get access to the menu sys-

tem

17. Press the right button to enter the Scene mode menu.

18. Using the four cursor buttons, navigate to the Flash Burst scene type

19. Select that scene type with the Menu/Set button

20. Aim camera at subject and compose picture generally

21. Hold down shutter button for burst of up to five flash shots

Take Picture Using Self-Timer

14. Place camera on tripod or other sturdy support

15. Turn Mode dial on top of the camera to the Intelligent Auto setting (letters iA in camera icon)

16. Press self-timer button (left cursor button)

17. Press Menu/Set button to select 10 Sec. setting

18. Use the Open button on top left of camera to pop up the built-in flash unit

19. Be sure camera is aimed properly at subjects

20. Press shutter button (and run around to be in the picture)

Record a High-Definition Motion Picture

14. Turn the Mode dial on top of the camera to the Motion Picture setting (film strip icon)

15. Set the Aspect Ratio switch on top of the lens barrel to 16:9

16. Press the Menu/Set button to get access to the Recording menu

17. Use the up or down cursor button to highlight Picture Mode

18. Press the right button to pop up the sub-menu

19. Highlight the HD setting

20. Select the HD setting with the Menu/Set button

21. Compose the picture

22. Press the shutter button to start the recording

23. Press the shutter button again to end the recording

Take Picture in Dimly Lit Place with Available Light (No Flash)

14. Turn the Mode dial on top of the camera to the SCN setting

15. Press the Menu/Set button to get access to the menu system

16. Press the right button to enter the Scene mode menu

17. Use the cursor buttons to navigate to the High Sens. setting

18. Press the Menu/Set button to select the High Sens. setting

19. Aim the camera at the subject and compose the picture

20. Press the shutter button to take the picture

Take Action Shots at Sporting Event

14. Turn the Mode dial on top of the camera to the SCN setting

15. Press the Menu/Set button to get access to the menu system

16. Press the right button to enter the Scene mode menu

17. Use the cursor buttons to navigate to the Sports setting

18. Press the Menu/Set button to select the Sports setting

19. Aim the camera at the subject and compose the picture

20. Press the shutter button to take the picture

Take Pictures Using Manual Exposure

14. Turn the Mode dial on top of the camera to the M setting.

15. Press joystick to the right to activate shutter speed selection, then press joystick up or down to select shutter speed.

16. Press joystick to the left to activate aperture selection, then press joystick up or down to select aperture.

17. If desired, press shutter button halfway down to see if EV scale is at zero, indicating proper exposure; adjust aperture or shutter speed if desired.

18. Press the shutter button to take the picture.

Play Back Pictures in the Camera

1. Set Record-playback switch, located at the right of the top of the LCD screen, to the lower position, for Playback

2. Turn the camera on with the On-off switch on the top right of the camera

3. Use the left and right cursor buttons to navigate backward and forward through the images in the camera

4. Press the Display button at the bottom left of the camera's back to show more or less information on the screen

Copy Photos to a Computer

1. Connect the smaller end of the supplied USB (computer data) cable to the center one of the three ports inside the little door on the right edge of the camera (held in shooting position)

2. Connect the larger end of the cable to the USB port on the computer (Windows or Macintosh)

3. The camera should show up on the computer as a drive name or letter

4. Double-click on the camera's icon and locate the folder called "DCIM."

5. Locate one or more folders inside that one. The first folder should be called 100_PANA.

6. Double-click on that folder or higher-numbered ones to open them.

204

7. Drag and drop images from those folders to the Pictures folder or other appropriate place(s) on the computer.

Appendix B
ACCESSORIES

When people buy a new camera, especially a fairly expensive model like the LX3, they often ask what accessories they should buy to go with it. The LX3 community is fortunate in that there are quite a few options available for this camera and its nearly identical sibling, the Leica D-Lux 4. I will hit the highlights, sticking mostly with items I have experience with. For information about a wide range of other accessories, including underwater housings, cable releases, digiscoping adapters, and other items, see the web sites listed in the Resources list later on. Two sites that have good lists of accessories are http://www.lx3-photography.com/ and http://leicarumors.com/leica-d-lux-4/.

Batteries

Here's one item for which you should go shopping either when you get the camera or right after. I use the camera pretty heavily, and I find it runs through batteries like a demon. You can't use disposable batteries, so if you're out taking pictures and the battery dies, you're out of luck unless you have a spare battery (or an AC adapter and a place to plug it in; see below). You don't necessarily have to buy a Panasonic-branded battery at a premium price; I found one of the Pearstone brand at a reasonable price.

You can also use batteries intended for the LX3's sister (nearly identical twin) camera, the Leica D-Lux 4, or replacements for that battery from other brands. The Leica battery's model

206

number is BP-DC4-U; the Panasonic battery's model number is CGA-S005; the Pearstone battery's model number is PE-CGAS005. There are undoubtedly other brands out there that will do just as well. However, you do need to use some caution and common sense; there are some "super-cheap" batteries that are not a good idea to use. I rely on the dealer's reputation to avoid shoddy merchandise in that sort of situation. I have had excellent online shopping experiences with B&H Photo-Video, 17th Street Photo, and Amazon.com, among others.

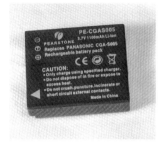

Cases

There are endless types of camera cases on the market. I like to keep a camera in a camera bag that has room for extra batteries, battery charger, connecting cables, the user's manual, flash, and other items. For my LX3, I got the Tamrac 5692, a small case that has room for the camera as well as an extra battery or other small items. This case has worked well as a convenient way to carry the camera, but there are probably hundreds of other cases available that would work just as well.

AC Adapter

The other alternative for powering the LX3 is the AC adapter. There is not too much to say about this accessory. I have used the Leica version, and it works well for what it does, in terms of providing a constant source of power to the camera. It consists of two parts: a small power brick attached to a thin cable ending in a small connector that plugs into the DC "in" port inside the little door on the right edge of the camera, and a standard-sized AC cord that you plug into the power brick and into an AC outlet.

The thin cable with brick is about five feet long; the AC cable is about six feet long, so the whole AC adapter assembly gives you about eleven feet of distance between the power outlet and the camera. I should emphasize that providing power to the camera is all this adapter does. It does not act as a battery charger, either for batteries outside of the camera or for batteries while they are installed in the camera. It is strictly a power source for the camera. It may be useful if you are doing extensive indoor work in a studio or laboratory setting, to eliminate the trouble of constantly charging batteries. For everyday applications, the AC adapter should not be considered a high-priority purchase.

Viewfinder

The LX3 does not come equipped with a viewfinder. There is no window for you to look through at eye level to compose your shot, as there is with a DSLR or with many rangefinder cameras. Nowadays you can find many small digital cameras that rely solely on the LCD screen for composition. Some photographers don't mind the lack of a viewfinder, and some find that lack unbearable. You can get an external viewfinder that fits into the hot shoe of the LX3 if you want one. Do you need an external viewfinder with the LX3? It's a matter of personal taste.

As for benefits, probably the main point weighing in favor of having a viewfinder is it lets you see clearly the scene the camera is aimed at, even in bad lighting conditions. For example, in bright sunlight, the LCD screen may be totally washed out, making it practically impossible to see the image on the screen well enough to compose the picture properly. Similarly, in dim light, it may be hard to make out the scene on the LCD. Another point in favor of a viewfinder is comfort in your shooting position. Some photographers prefer to hold the camera up to their face and look through a little window when composing a shot. This may be from years of habit, or it may help them hold the camera steadier by bracing it against their forehead. The preference for a viewfinder may also have something to do with tradition; a person may feel more like a traditional photographer when using a viewfinder to evaluate the picture before pressing the shutter button. Finally, if you use a viewfinder rather than the LCD screen, you can turn off the D-Lux 4's screen, thereby saving battery power and extending the number of images you can record before changing batteries.

On the other side of the coin, the LCD screen provides a considerable amount of information, such as shutter speed, shooting mode, flash mode, etc., that the viewfinders available for the LX3 do not. (Though you could use the LCD screen to see that information and still use the viewfinder for composition.) Also, it may be possible to take candid pictures without detection more readily with the LCD screen, because you can casually aim the camera from waist level rather than holding it up to your eye. If you do get a viewfinder, one problem is that you cannot use any other accessory that uses the hot shoe, such as an external flash unit, at the same time. The viewfinder is light and easy to remove, though, so you can switch it out with the flash or other accessory.

There is one viewfinder that is designed specifically for the LX3: the Panasonic DMW-VF1, pictured above on the camera. It is a compact unit that weighs only about half an ounce (about 16 grams). Its design integrates with that of the camera, and it does not obstruct the camera's Mode dial or the pop-up flash unit (though the flash comes breathtakingly close to it when it pops up). It does give a clear view of the scene you aim at, and it has well defined lines in the view that show the outline for the camera's standard wide-angle view at the 24mm equivalent focal length.

The main drawback of the Panasonic viewfinder is its cost. At this writing, a new one sells for about $150.00, which, while about half the cost of the equivalent model for the Leica D-Lux 4, still seems like a lot of money for a tiny item that does nothing but sit on top of the camera with no electronics or moving parts. Some users of this camera use viewfinders made by Voigtlander, Contax, and other companies, though some of those block the flash unit.

Cable Release and Adapter

Some higher-end digital cameras come equipped with (or can be equipped with) wired or wireless remote controls that allow you to trigger the shutter from a distance and without exerting any pressure on the camera itself. This system can be of great benefit when you're using a long shutter speed to photograph a nighttime scene or in any situation when you don't want to risk jiggling the camera.

There is no remote control available for the LX3 that I'm aware of, but there is an ingenious custom-made adapter that lets you use an old-fashioned (but still effective) cable release. This device, sold by the Lensmate company (http://www.lensmateonline.com) is very well made and works beautifully. It slips firmly into the hotshoe, and the cable release screws neatly into the hold that sits directly above the shutter button. You can use any length of cable release that you want. I have found this system to be very effective when I need to tread lightly in my shooting.

Add-on Filters and Lenses

There is no way to attach a filter or other add-on item, such as a close-up lens, direcly to the lens of the LX3. In order to add such accessory items, you need to get an adapter. The adapter is like a short extension tube. You have to unscrew the thin trim ring from the camera's lens, and set it aside in a safe place.

The adapter then screws onto the exposed threads. You can then screw onto the end of the adaptor any filter or accessory that fits onto the adapter you're using. As I discussed earlier in the Infrared section, I have used an adapter from Lensmate (shown below with infrared filter) that accepts 46mm screw-on filters.

There are other options available. Panasonic makes an adapter, model number DMW-LA4. I have seen an adapter advertised by West Coast Cameras on its web site at http://www.west-coastcameras.com. Leica does not sell an adapter.

Once you have the adapter, you may want to try a UV (ultra-violet) filter, a neutral density filter, an infrared filter, a po-larizer, or others, depending on your needs and interests. I

212

have used Panasonic's own Wide Conversion Lens, pictured below, which converts the normal 24mm wide-angle lens to an 18mm lens at its widest setting. It yields good results, but the relatively small additional width may not be worth the effort of attaching this fairly bulky add-on lens.

I also have used the Opteka 0.20x Fisheye attachment, which gives the distorted circular effect characterstic of such lenses. That attachment requires a different-sized adaptor tube, but it comes with that tube. (At least, when I bought mine it did). This attachment is inexpensive and not of the finest quality, but it can give you the unusual fisheye look, as shown below.

External Flash

Whether to buy an external flash unit is going to be very much a question of how you will use the LX3. For everyday Intelligent Autos that are not taken at long distances, the built-in flash should suffice. It works automatically with the camera's exposure controls to expose the images well, and it is even capable of taking short bursts of flash exposures. It is limited by its low power, though. If you are planning to use the camera to take photos of groups of people in large spaces, or otherwise need additional power or features, there are some options. There are several models of flash sold by Panasonic that will work with the LX3. The smallest of these is the Panasonic DMW-FL220, pictured below, which fits very well with the camera in terms of looks and function. The unit fits into the camera's hot shoe and extends slightly less than 4 inches (about 9.5 cm) above the camera. It weighs about 5.7 ounces (160 g) with batteries. It provides more power than the built-in flash (its range at ISO 100 is about 22 meters or 72 feet), and communicates automatically with the camera in the same ways that the built-in flash does.

The main drawback with the FL220 is that it is a single unit with no rotating flash head, although its head is pointed slightly upwards. However, there is no possibility of changing the angle of the flash. It does come with a diffuser screen that snaps in place over the flash head, and you could rig up some sort of deflector yourself, but it may hamper your ability to achieve the best results to have a rigid unit that cannot have its flash head rotated in any way.

There are two larger flash units sold by Panasonic that should work well with the LX3: the DMW-FL360 and the DMW-FL500, which have guide numbers of 36 meters (118 feet) and 50 meters (164 feet), respectively.

Another possibility for a fully automatic external flash unit is the Metz Mecablitz 48 AF-1, in the version for Olympus/Panasonic cameras. Again, like the Panasonic models discussed above, this unit functions just like the built-in flash in terms of communicating with the camera for functions such as flash output and exposure control. Also, like the larger Panasonic units, it has a flash head that rotates up to a vertical position, aiming at the ceiling, so you can bounce the flash at various angles. And, of course, it is considerably more powerful than the built-in flash or the smaller external Panasonic units: The Metz unit has a guide number of 48 meters, or 157 feet.

215

The only drawback to this unit is its size. It is not excessively tall; when aimed horizontally at the subject, it extends only about 5 inches (12.5 cm) above the camera, as opposed to 4 inches (9.5 cm) for the FL220, but it weighs about 15.6 ounces (440 g), almost three times as much as the FL220, and, in fact, considerably more than the camera itself, which weighs slightly more than 9 ounces (260 g). When I hold the camera with the Metz flashs attached, the whole assembly feels overbalanced by the flash. However, it is an excellent flash unit, and if you need the power and the flexibility that comes from having a rotating flash head, then this unit would be a good purchase.

One final note about flash. If you get the Metz unit, it comes with a hinged diffuser that fits over the flash head; the Olympus flash also comes with a built-in slide-on diffuser. If you're using the Panasonic FL220 or the LX3's built-in flash, though, you're on your own. Some enterprising users have devised their own home-built diffusers. One possibility I've heard about but haven't tried personally is to take a translucent white plastic 35mm film can and squeeze it over the pop-up flash. Others have tried a ping-pong ball with part cut out. You also could try a white handkerchief or tissue paper. If you want a commercial product, one that I have found to be useful is the Mini Softbox from RPS Studio, which folds flat when not in use, and attaches with velcro flaps over many flash units

Appendix C
Resources for Further Information
Photography Books

A visit to any large general bookstore or a search on Amazon.com will reveal the vast assortment of books about digital photography that is currently available. Rather than trying to compile a long bibliography, I will list the few books that I consulted while writing this guide.

J. Canfield, *Camera Raw 101* (Amphoto Books 2009)

D. Pogue, *Digital Photography: The Missing Manual* (O'Reilly Media, Inc., 2009)

C. George, *Mastering Digital Flash Photography* (Lark Books, 2008)

C. Harnischmacher, *Closeup Shooting* (Rocky Nook, 2007)

J. Paduano, *The Art of Infrared Photography* (4th ed., Amherst Media, 1998)

J. Gulbins and R. Gulbins, *Photographic Multishot Techniques* (Rocky Nook 2009).

Web Sites

At this writing there are quite a few web sites with information about the Panasonic Lumix DMC-LX3 and its nearly-identical twin, the Leica D-Lux 4. Since web sites come and go and change their addresses, it's impossible to compile a list that will be accurate far into the future. One way to find the latest sites is to use a good search engine such as Google or Bing and type in "Lumix LX3." I just did so in Google and got 286,000 hits.

Another approach can be to go to Amazon.com, search for the product, and read the users' reviews, though you have to be careful to weed out the people who are disgruntled for reasons that don't have anything to do with the product itself. You can also visit a reputable dealer's site, such as that of B&H Photo Video, and read the users' reviews of the camera there. I will include below a list of some of the sites or links I have found useful, with the caveat that some of them may not be accessible by the time you read this.

Guy Parsons' Web Site

http://homepages.ihug.com.au/~parsog/panasonic/01-intro.html

An excellent site with a miscellany of information about the LX3.

Digital Photography Review

http://forums.dpreview.com/forums/forum.asp?forum=1033

http://forums.dpreview.com/forums/forum.asp?forum=1038
These are the current web addresses for the "Panasonic Talk"

forum and the "Leica Talk" forum within the dpreview.com site. Dpreview.com is one of the most established and authoritative sites for reviews, discussion forums, technical information, and other resources concerning digital cameras.

Camera Labs Review

http://www.cameralabs.com/reviews/Panasonic_Lumix_ DMC_LX3/index.shtml

This link points to another thorough review of the Panasonic Lumix LX3, including a video tour of the camera and its features.

Imaging Resource Review

http://www.imaging-resource.com/PRODS/LX3/LX3A.HTM

This link points to another web site's review of the LX3.

The Official Panasonic Site

http://www2.panasonic.com/consumer-electronics/support/ Cameras-Camcorders/Digital-Cameras/Lumix-Digital-Cameras/model.DMC-LX3K

This link is to the official Panasonic site's information about the LX3.

The Official Leica Site

The United States arm of the Leica company provides resources on its site, including the downloadable version of the user's manual for the D-Lux 4 and other technical information.

http://us.leica-camera.com/photography/compact_cameras/d-lux_4

http://us.leica-camera.com/service/downloads/compact_cameras/d-lux_4/index.html

Leica Rumors

The "Leica Rumors" site includes a page dedicated to the D-Lux 4 which compiles excellent information about accessories and other resources for the camera.

http://leicarumors.com/leica-d-lux-4/

The Leica Camera Forum

This site hosts a discussion forum about all Leica cameras, including the D-Lux 4.

http://www.l-camera-forum.com/leica-forum/digital-forum/

Leica FAQ

A compilation of practical and technical notes about the D-Lux 4 by an Australian photographer.

http://nemeng.com/leica/010f.shtml

Infrared Photography

This site provides some helpful information about infrared photography with digital cameras.

http://www.wroniak.net/photo/infrared/

Digiscoping

The following sites provide information about equipment and techniques for digiscoping with the D-Lux 4 and Leica spotting scopes.

http://leicabirding.blogspot.com/2009/06/digiscoping-yet-another-review.html

http://us.leica-camera.com/sport_optics/televid_spotting_scopes/digiscoping/

Other Information About the LX3

The Panasonic site listed below provides the downloadable user's manual. The other two sites listed also provide information about the Panasonic camera.

http://service.us.panasonic.com/OPERMANPDF/DMCLX3.PDF

http://www.lx3-photography.com

http://www.luminous-landsape.com/reviews/cameras/lx3.shtml

Lensmate

This is the site for Lensmate, a company that sells accessories for the LX3 and the D-Lux 4, including an adaptor for filters and add-on lenses.

http://www.lensmateonline.com

Index

R

S

CPSIA information can be obtained
at www.ICGtesting.com
Printed in the USA
253405LV00001B